Railway Memories

NORTHALLE
RIPON &
WENSLEYDALE

Stephen Chapman

BELLCODE BOOKS
21 DALE AVENUE
TODMORDEN WEST YORKSHIRE OL14 6BA
email: bellcode4books@yahoo.co.uk

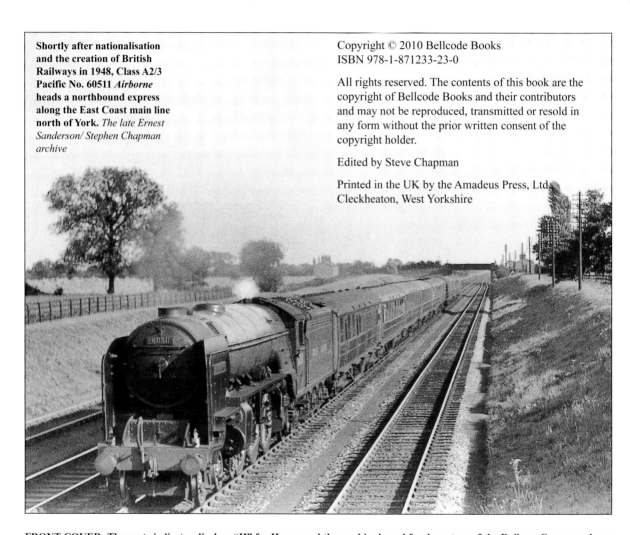

Shortly after nationalisation and the creation of British Railways in 1948, Class A2/3 Pacific No. 60511 *Airborne* **heads a northbound express along the East Coast main line north of York.** *The late Ernest Sanderson/ Stephen Chapman archive*

Copyright © 2010 Bellcode Books
ISBN 978-1-871233-23-0

All rights reserved. The contents of this book are the copyright of Bellcode Books and their contributors and may not be reproduced, transmitted or resold in any form without the prior written consent of the copyright holder.

Edited by Steve Chapman

Printed in the UK by the Amadeus Press, Ltd, Cleckheaton, West Yorkshire

FRONT COVER: The route indicator displays "H" for Hawes and the road is cleared for departure of the Railway Correspondence & Travel Society railtour, so all the gricers on the track at the north end of Northallerton station must hurry back on board if they are not to be left behind. The date is Saturday 25th April 1964 and this special from Leeds, hauled by B16 4-6-0 No. 61435 of Hull Dairycoates, was the last passenger train to Hawes as the Wensleydale line closed completely beyond Redmire with effect from the following Monday. The train is standing on what the summer 1960 Working Timetable described as the "Slow Platform" and the 1968-1969 Working Timetable as the "Loop Platform." *Jack Wild/Stephen Chapman archive*

BACK COVER TOP: A1 Pacific No. 60151 *Midlothian* saunters past the 1843 Great North of England Railway cottages at Pilmoor with a rather short northbound fitted freight in 1965. The stone plaques proclaiming their GNER origin can be clearly seen between the upstairs windows. The 1930s pagoda-roof Pilmoor South signal box is in the right distance. *Neville Stead*

BACK COVER BOTTOM: It is April 1977 and the branch line pick-up goods lives on in Wensleydale. With Leyburn station and goods yard in the left background and Leyburn East signal box on the right, Brush Type 4 No. 47287 prepares for the return run to Northallerton. *Malcolm Roughley/Stephen Chapman archive*

FRONTISPIECE: Looking at this scene, it seems incredible that Ripon has had no railway whatsoever since 1969. Here, in the late 1920s or early 1930s, no lesser locomotive than London & North Eastern Railway No. 2404 *City of Ripon*, one of the Pacifics built by the North Eastern Railway to the design of Sir Vincent Raven in 1920, calls at Ripon with a northbound express. *Neville Stead collection*

Thanks are due to all those who have so willingly provided material and assistance for this edition of Railway Memories including Robert Anderson, Ken Appleby, Rev. David Benson, Ron Hollier, Alan Thompson, the North Eastern Railway Association, and the staff of North Yorkshire County Archive and Northallerton Reference Library Local Studies. **Information for this book** about the 1950s and later has come mainly from original sources, especially British Railways documents, but for historical information we acknowledge the following: Regional History of Railways North East England by Ken Hoole; Railways in the Yorkshire Dales by Ken Hoole(Dalesman,) The Wensleydale Railway by C.S. Hallas(Dalesman,) BR Steam Shed Allocations by P.B. Hands; contemporary editions of Modern Railways, Railnews, Railway Magazine,The Railway Observer and Trains Illustrated.

INTRODUCTION

The Vale of York, Vale of Mowbray and Wensleydale may be among the more agricultural and less densely populated parts of Yorkshire but the railways that once criss-crossed them had a richness and diversity that was hard to match.

Today, all that remains of them are the East Coast main line reaching from York to the one-time main line crossroads of Northallerton and on to Scotland, the old Leeds Northern from Northallerton to Teesside, and the truncated 22-mile remnant of the Wensleydale lifeline that once crossed the country from east to west. But within the lifetimes of many of us, railways spread across the region to Ripon, Masham, Hawes, Baldersby and Topcliffe, Easingwold and the centre of Thirsk.

It says something about the wealth of operational interest of the railways in this rural area that they once possessed no less than six locomotive turntables.

Railway Memories No. 23 recalls the time when passenger trains hauled by vintage locomotives ran all the way from Northallerton to the Settle & Carlisle line at Garsdale, when express trains including one of the nation's most prestigious Pullman trains served or passed through Britain's 4th smallest city which has had no railway since 1969, when meandering branch lines - including one of the few passenger railways to escape the 1923 Grouping or 1948 nationalisation - connected small market towns to the outside world, and when Pacifics and Deltics ruled the East Coast main line.

Contents

Page 4   **Setting the scene**

Page 28   **The Great North of England & Easingwold**

Page 52   **The Leeds Northern & Masham**

Page 84   **A journey through Wensleydale**

On 7th September 1964 British Railways began using the 24-hour clock in its working timetables so we use am and pm up to that date and thereafter the 24-hour clock except where direct comparisons are made between times in different eras.

Finally, special tribute must be paid to the late James Hague of Ripon who so comprehensively recorded the 1950s North Yorkshire railway scene and without whose dedicated work this Railway Memories might not have happened.

Change at Northallerton. The north end of the station in early 1954 where new BR Standard Class 3 2-6-0 No.77001 waits in the Slow line platform with a northbound stopping train and J21 0-6-0 No. 65038 on a Wensleydale service boils up nicely in the bay. Within weeks, passenger trains will have ceased running into Wensleydale and before much longer the BR Standards will have replaced the old NER locos at most of the region's branch line outposts. *Neville Stead collection*

Setting the scene

The Vale of York, that wide tract of level, fertile land which lies between the Yorkshire Wolds and North Yorkshire Moors in the east and the Pennines in the west, is predominantly agricultural and relatively lightly populated.

With no great industrial development, its principal railways were built to move goods and people through the vale as swiftly as possible on their way between the rapidly developing and heavily populated West Riding and North East regions. Branch lines served those market towns that were off the main routes, such as Boroughbridge, Easingwold and Masham, while potential business from tourism, minerals and dairy produce made a branch into Wensleydale a priority for the early railway builders.

In a 1920s pamphlet for the London & North Eastern Railway, C.B. Fawcett, B.Litt., Reader in Geography at Leeds University, described the Vale of York as "the wide and continuous lowland which occupies the centre of Yorkshire from north to south for 60 miles. In the south it is about 30 miles wide, but north of York it gradually narrows till it is a little less than half that width in the Northallerton Gate[the gap between hills in the east and hills in the west which connects the Vale of York with the North East.] Its surface slopes very gently from north to south....A large part of the soil in the Vale is very fertile, though there are barren patches of glacial sands and some peat deposits, and it is one of the chief agricultural districts in England. The population is spread over it fairly evenly in small villages and market towns with a mean density which almost everywhere exceeds 50 per square mile(an accompanying chart showed population in the centre to be under 100 per square mile and 100 to 500 per square mile along the east and west margins-*sic*.) Towards the edges of the vale the ground is somewhat higher, and the freedom from floods, together with the better water supply from the hills, has led to a slight concentration of population, which makes the margins more populous than the centre."

During world war two the vale's flat topography was ideal for the location of airforce bases which provided extra business for local stations. Some to the north of York, such as Dishforth, Topcliffe, Linton-on-Ouse and Leeming, remained operational after the war and still do so at the time of writing in some form or another with either the RAF or the Army.

Of the Pennine uplands west of the vale, C.B. Fawcett wrote: "...the central parts are mostly formed of outcrops of rocks of the Carboniferous limestone series.." Noting that unlike the Pennines between West Yorkshire and Lancashire where deep valleys enable a railway to pass up one valley and reach the head of a similar valley on the other side by a long but comparatively low level tunnel, avoiding severe gradients, he wrote: "further north the highland is too wide to be easily tunnelled, the lines via Hawes and Stainmore climb over the highland and cross by passes at much higher levels."

Railways first entered the vale north of York in 1841 when the Great North of England Railway completed its main line from York to Croft, just south of Darlington. There it would soon join the Newcastle & Darlington Junction Railway and form a continuous route to Tyneside. The GNER was virtually straight and level throughout and needed few civil engineering works, the largest between York and Northallerton being a bridge over the River Ouse on the outskirts of York. It passed along the west side of Northallerton and missed Thirsk by only a mile and a half, the racecourse separating the two. It eventually became part of the East Coast main line(ECML) from London King's Cross to Edinburgh but even upon its opening, the developing national rail network already made train travel possible from Northallerton and Thirsk to London(Euston) by way of York, Derby and Birmingham.

By 1845 the so-called Railway King, George Hudson, had taken a lease on the GNER which a year later merged with the Newcastle & Darlington Junction Railway to become the York & Newcastle Railway which, upon subsequent extension to the Scottish border, was renamed the York, Newcastle & Berwick.

The first of the small market towns to be connected with the new main line was Boroughbridge to which the York & Newcastle completed a branch in June 1847. It was to have been on a GNER main line to Leeds but Hudson had this scheme withdrawn to clear the way for the Leeds & Thirsk Railway. The branch joined the main line at a remote spot just under seven miles south of Thirsk where a station was built purely to facilitate connections with main line trains, and so Pilmoor was established. Just about the only residents in the area were railway workers and their families occupying a row of cottages built on the Up side in 1843 and still bearing stone plaques with the legend "GNER Co. 1843" to this day. The railway company even set up its own oil-gas works at Pilmoor(as it did at Northallerton and Thirsk) in the 19th century to serve its isolated community, plus a siding for delivering coal and provisions to the cottages.

The GNER acquired powers to build a branch from its main line by means of a Darlington-facing junction at Castle Hills(just north of Northallerton station) across the Vale of Mowbray to Bedale. The section to the Great North Road at Leeming Lane(later known as Leeming Bar) was completed by the York, Newcastle & Berwick in March 1848. But then came Hudson's fall from grace and the collapse of his railway empire, and work on the branch stopped.

The GNER and its successors weren't the only companies aiming to connect the populous regions of Yorkshire with the North East. The afore-mentioned Leeds & Thirsk was building its line between the two via Harrogate and Ripon, the Ripon-Thirsk section opening in 1848 with the whole route being completed in July 1849. The Ripon-Thirsk section passed through only slightly more demanding countryside than the YN&B's York-Northallerton line, its main civil engineering features being at Ripon, namely the viaduct over the River Ure immediately south of the station together embankments and bridges over the River Skell and Ripon Canal. A bridge was also needed to carry the line over the River Swale east of Baldersby. At its northern end, the line crossed over the YN&B

The Great North of England Railway's main line from York to the north was almost straight and level throughout making it a race-track for the country's fastest trains. Here, one of Sir Nigel Gresley's celebrated A4 Pacifics, No. 60031 *Golden Plover*, forges round the slight curve at Pasture Field House, north of Thirsk, with The Elizabethan at 1.8pm on 23rd June 1961 during its 393-mile non-stop run from King's Cross to Edinburgh. *Roy Wood/Peter Rose collection*

to terminate in Thirsk itself but in order to meet the company's aspiration of running trains through to the North East, a curve was laid down to the YN&B station.

In 1852 the Leeds & Thirsk extended its network by completing the line from a junction at Melmerby, three miles north of Ripon, direct to Northallerton where it passed under the YN&B, and from Northallerton(on the YN&B) to Stockton-on-Tees. In recognition of its ambitions, the Leeds & Thirsk changed its name to the Leeds Northern in 1851. But the Melmerby-Northallerton section was nothing more than a single track branch carrying only a local service while the company still ran its principal trains via Thirsk.

In May 1853 Pilmoor acquired increased junction status when the YN&B's Thirsk & Malton line was completed, leaving the York-Darlington main line south of the station to head east via Coxwold and Gilling.

A year later the York, Newcastle & Berwick and the Leeds Northern merged with the York & North Midland to form the mighty North Eastern Railway and all the existing lines in the area came under that one company.

In 1856 the NER extended Hudson's truncated Wensleydale line to Bedale where it met the independent Bedale & Leyburn Railway, founded by local interests eager to see the line progress after Hudson's downfall. The 10-mile B&L opened to goods traffic in November 1855 with passenger services following in May 1856. It was absorbed by the NER in 1859.

The 1860s saw the formulation of a scheme to build a through railway from Leeds to Scarborough which avoided York by incorporating the existing Boroughbridge and Thirsk & Malton lines. To this end, the Boroughbridge branch was to be made a through route to Knaresborough while a line was built over the ECML south of Pilmoor to connect it with the Thirsk & Malton. But then came the sort of economic downturn we are all too familiar with nowadays and the scheme was dropped. The section connecting the Boroughbridge and Malton lines was never used, the track removed by the 1880s and the trackbed used for locomens eyesight tests. The Boroughbridge-Knaresborough section was completed but not until 1875. Meanwhile, a York-facing curve onto the Malton line, from Bishophouse Junction to Sunbeck Junction, was opened in 1871, enabling the operation of a direct York-Pickering service(see Railway Memories No.19.)

It is worth recalling at this point that during the 1840s Railway Mania a number of rather grand-sounding schemes for through routes linking the West Riding and Lancashire with not only the North East but also western Scotland that would have passed through Wensleydale were from time to time banded about. They included the Yorkshire & Glasgow Union Railway (Thirsk-Bedale-Hawes-Kirkby Stephen-Penrith,) the Liverpool, Manchester & Newcastle-upon-Tyne Railway, and the Manchester, Liverpool and Great North of England Union Railway. Another batch such as the Skipton, Wharfedale & Leyburn Junction Railway followed in the 1860s. None made it to reality but they did indirectly accelerate the extension of

On the original main line of the Leeds & Thirsk Railway between Thirsk and Melmerby in the 1940s, one of the NER's elegant and useful D20 4-4-0s, No. 2384 of the LNER, heads a Thirsk to Leeds stopping train past the crossing with the A1 road at Leeming Lane(not to be confused with Leeming Lane on the Wensleydale branch.) Following doubling and upgrading of the direct Melmerby-Northallerton route in 1901, this section was left to handle little more than local traffic. *J.W. Hague/Neville Stead collection*

the local network. The proposed Northern Counties Union Railway authorized in 1846 was to run from Melmerby to Hawes and some earthworks were begun at the south end, some of which were eventually incorporated in the Leeds & Thirsk's Melmerby-Northallerton extension. A later attempt at a similar line, the Hawes & Melmerby Railway - which the NER encouraged by taking a half share in order to stave off incursions by certain fancifully-named companies - also came to nothing and was rendered unnecessary by the NER's westerly progress through Wensleydale, the Leyburn-Askrigg section opening in February 1873. To compensate for the loss of the Leyburn-Melmerby portion, the NER built the branch from Melmerby to Masham which it opened in July 1875.

Three years later, on 1st October 1878, the Wensleydale line was finally completed when the NER opened the Askrigg-Hawes section, and the Midland Railway the five and three quarter miles from Hawes to Hawes Junction(later renamed Garsdale) on its Settle & Carlisle line, opened in 1876. As with Pilmoor, there was no community at Garsdale but for a scattering of farms and cottages for railway staff and the station was built for the purpose of interchange between the Hawes branch and the Settle & Carlisle. The Midland also built Hawes station which was a joint enterprise while the NER ran the passenger service throughout. The Midland granted the NER

running powers along the S&C to Settle Junction and the NER granted the Midland running powers to Leyburn, though neither is thought to have used them on a regular basis. Upon completion, the Wensleydale branch formed another trans-Pennine route but it never developed any degree of through traffic. Instead, it enabled the considerable local traffic to be worked into and out of the dale from either end. In 1882, operation was made easier by completion of a curve leading on to the branch from Northallerton station, removing the need for trains to reverse at Castle Hills. This subsequently became the main route to the branch, the section to Castle Hills being used mainly for exchange of goods wagons.

The Wensleydale branch was very different to the main lines through the area whose purpose was to speed passengers and goods as quickly as possible from one region of Britain to another, local needs being almost incidental. Wensleydale may have been remote and isolated but within its physical confines it had a healthy local economy based on sheep and dairy farming as well as quarrying, with bustling livestock and general produce markets. The railway enabled it to break out from the boundaries which geography had imposed. In fact, there is no better example of how railways and steam overturned society from a collection of peasant communities held back by isolation from each other into the commercially interconnected world we know today.

With the benefit of lush pastures, Wensleydale's farmers produced excellent milk - and lots of it but they were too far from anywhere to sell it beyond their own locality. In the time it took by horse and cart it would have gone off before it got to any centre of population. They had to convert it into a product that would keep and so the famous Wensleydale cheese came about. As the industrial revolution gained momentum, some farmers got round the problem of distance by setting up cow sheds in such growing cities as Manchester where cows were kept like battery hens. With no pasture, they were filthy, contaminated places. Cows and milk became infected, spreading illness to humans and probably tuberculosis. Also, to supply the dale with fresh stock, cattle had to be driven over rough tracks and moors - there were no proper roads then - suffering damaged limbs and arriving lame.

Then came the railway. Suddenly, farmers could send fresh milk overnight to mass markets as far away as London and the dale prospered. Also, stock could now be brought into and out of the dale quickly and injury-free. A similar situation applied to the dale's quarrying activities. Whereas stone could only be used locally for building, limestone could now be sold and transported in bulk to a ready-made market on Teesside where it was in demand as a flux for the iron furnaces. And as prosperity and leisure time grew among the populace, tourists came by train to enjoy the dale's outstanding beauty, starting a whole new industry.

Unlike most other cross-Pennine routes, the Wensleydale line required relatively few great engineering structures, although it reached 750ft above sea level by the time it got to Hawes and then climbed along cuttings and embankments to 1000ft above sea level in the 5.75 miles from Hawes to Garsdale. This stretch included the line's only tunnel, just 245 yards long at Mossdale Head. A four-arch stone viaduct was also needed to cross the gorge scoured out by Mossdale beck while five-arch Appersett Viaduct was the first structure encountered west of Hawes. Other notable features were iron bridges over the River Ure east of Hawes and the Swale west of Ainderby.

By the 1880s only one town in the Vale of York was still without a railway. Easingwold had been left out because the York-Darlington main line passed two and a half miles to the west so local interests formed the independent Easingwold Railway which connected the town with the ECML at Alne station. Opened on 25th July 1891 it remained entirely independent throughout its 66-year life, even escaping nationalisation in 1948.

Upon completion of the Easingwold Railway, the main line network in the Vales of York and Mowbray and Wensleydale had reached its peak although changes, particularly to the layout at Northallerton, were to follow in order to improve operational efficiency.

One other railway in the area was the 2ft-gauge system which

The terrain at the west end of the Wensleydale line was as rugged as it was gentle at the east end, the line climbing to 1000ft above sea level by the time it reached Garsdale. The most impressive of its few major structures was the five-arch Appersett Viaduct west of Hawes where the line also had a distinctly London Midland flavour, having been built by the Midland Railway as an extension of its Settle & Carlisle line. Hellifield-based Ivatt Class 2 2-6-2 tank No. 41205 heads three probably almost empty coaches through spectacular scenery while working the afternoon Hawes-Garsdale service. *J.W. Hague/Neville Stead collection*

climbed from Masham up to reservoir construction sites in Colsterdale. The line was built in 1905 for the construction of Harrogate Corporation's Roundhill reservoir. When that was completed in 1910 it was taken over by Leeds Corporation for construction of its neighbouring Leighton reservoir. Work on that was held up by the first world war(during which time the workmen's huts were used as a prisoner of war camp and the line used for supplies.) Abandoned by the mid-1920s following the completion of Leighton reservoir, it began from a construction yard across the road from Masham station to which the NER laid a siding from its own goods yard. The NER's branch approached Masham station by a 1 in 61 falling gradient and on one occasion a goods train ran away, careered across the road and came to grief in the yard.

During world war two a double track emergency line was laid between the low level Leeds Northern at Romanby Gates, below the west side of Northallerton station, and the ECML at Castle Hills which could be quickly brought into use to keep trains running should the ECML through the station be blocked by enemy action. It crossed the curve giving direct access between Northallerton station and the Wensleydale branch neither low enough for a bridge nor high enough for a flat crossing so a novel trolley bridge was devised which could be run into position should the emergency line be needed. It wasn't needed and the line and all its apparatus were removed after the war.

Passenger services

Some of the most famous express trains in the world have passed through Northallerton and Thirsk on their way between London and Scotland - the Flying Scotsman, The Silver Jubilee, The Elizabethan, The Queen of Scots, The Aberdonian, and The Heart of Midlothian to name a few.

In 1935 a new and glorious era for ECML passenger trains began which continues to this day. That was when the LNER introduced Sir Nigel Gresley's streamlined high speed expresses powered by his illustrious A4 Pacifics. The first of them was the Newcastle-King's Cross Silver Jubilee, so-named to celebrate King George V's 25 years reign. The streamlined A4s continued to head the route's premier expresses until June 1962 when the 22 Deltic diesels took over the work of 55 Pacifics. That may have appeared to be the end of the streamlined era but the 3,300hp Deltics were the world's most powerful single unit diesel locomotives and could eat up mile upon mile at an uninterrupted 100mph. Aided by appropriate track and signalling improvements they slashed steam journey times in a way that other diesels - namely the English Electric Type 4s - could not when introduced in the late 1950s. The Deltics continued to roar along the ECML until the end of 1981 but in 1978 British Rail introduced its InterCity 125 high speed diesel trains(full timetable coming into effect on 8th May) which raced along the route at 125mph with even more spectacular cuts in journey times - and the streamlined era was back. They

The Easingwold Railway remained wholly independent throughout its 66-year life but in later years it hired its motive power from British Railways. In 1948 and with the passenger service about to end, J71 0-6-0T No. 68294 stands at Easingwold platform with a venerable six-wheeled coach while a horse box occupies the adjacent loading dock. *E.E. Smith/Neville Stead collection*

Between 1961 and 1978 the 3,300hp Deltics brought the only break in the operation of streamlined trains on prime East Coast main line expresses since the mid-1930s, but they were nevertheless more than worthy successors to the Pacifics they replaced. With the Deltic era almost over and streamlined InterCity 125 trains taking over the premier services, No. 55005 *The Prince of Wales's Own Regiment of Yorkshire* does the ton as it roars past the London-Edinburgh half-way point on 16th April 1979. Its train is an Inter-City service to King's Cross which had started at Berwick due to the collapse of Penmansheil Tunnel in Scotland. *Neville Stead*

were the world's fastest diesel trains - just as the A4 *Mallard* was the world's fastest steam loco. When electrification was completed in 1991 a new breed of streamlined express came into service, the InterCity 225 powered by Class 91 electric locomotives, still running at 125mph but capable of 140 if signalling systems had permitted. In 2010 both the 125s and 225s operate the East Coast services but they are joined by other streamlined trains. Since 2002 the 125mph Voyager and the tilting Super Voyager diesel units have been used on Cross-Country expresses between Newcastle, Birmingham, the South West and the South Coast, racing up and down the NE main line north of York at the rate of two each way an hour during daytime.

The East Coast main line's high speed expresses shot through Northallerton and Thirsk with barely a glance. The summer 1960 working timetable showed around 50 ECML passenger trains each way through Northallerton(including those that called there but not those which travelled via Ripon) every 24 hours on weekdays. On top of those were quite a number of trains which ran on only one or two days a week. Some trains which travelled via Stockton avoided Northallerton station by taking the low level line via Boroughbridge Road and Longlands Junction.

There may be far more daytime ECML passenger trains in 2010 but at the start of the 1960s there was the most amazing variety. Amongst the usual expresses between King's Cross, Newcastle and Scotland, the North East-South West/South Coast expresses, and the Newcastle-Liverpool Trans-Pennine trains, were regular timetabled troop trains to and from Catterick Camp, Leeds-York-Newcastle trains(including Metro-Cammel diesel multiple units complete with buffet cars,) York-

Stockton-West Hartlepool local trains, Colchester-Newcastle and Glasgow trains, a Liverpool Exchange-Newcastle express, boat trains to and from the Tyne Commission Quay for ferries to Scandinavia, overnight sleeping car services and York-Inverness, Exeter-Newcastle, Newcastle-Dover and Marylebone-Perth car sleeper trains - and even a Saltburn-King's Cross express. The main line was just as busy with passenger traffic at night as during the day - if not more so. It is incredible to think that in 2009 there was not a single passenger service on this section of the ECML between approximately 01.15 and 05.30, all overnight seated and sleeper trains having been switched to the West Coast main line 22 years before. Also in summer 1960 there were nine Down and six Up dedicated parcels, mail, newspaper and empty stock trains each weekday 24 hours. By 2009 there were none at all - there being no appreciable degree of parcels traffic left on conventional trains(as opposed to intermodal) while the few mail trains that remained had all been on the West Coast since 2004.

None of the ECML's legendary named expresses stopped at Northallerton or Thirsk but anyone prepared to spend 21 hours at Northallerton station in, say, summer 1957 could witness the passage of no less than 32 titled trains almost around the clock - almost certainly hauled by Pacifics and all but two using the York-Darlington section of the ECML but with three to be seen only on certain days of the week. In the dead of night were the principal sleeping car trains, the first to come thundering through at around 11.30pm being The Aberdonian, the 7pm from King's Cross. About 20 minutes later would pass the 10.35pm Newcastle-King's Cross sleeper - The Tynesider. Then, in the space of 20 minutes between 2 and 2.30am came the Up and Down Night Scotsman - the 10.15pm King's Cross-

When it comes to railways, there will always be an exception to whatever is stated. In steam days East Coast expresses normally seared through Northallerton at between 65 and 80mph but here the most famous of them all, under the charge of new and yet to be named A1 Pacific No. 60158, has been brought to a stand in platform 3 some time around 1950. The reason is unknown but clearly it is not a stop for passengers as all the carriage doors are shut and no-one is on the platform apart from the two chaps conversing with the driver. Doubtless this was a signal stop but why the Great Eastern-style headcode discs - had it been diverted via Cambridge earlier in its journey? The 10am King's Cross-Edinburgh ran on Sundays, still non-stop to Newcastle but slower and un-named.
Neville Stead collection

Dundee and 8.35pm Dundee-King's Cross, neither of which made any passenger stops between London and Edinburgh. About 20 minutes behind the Up train was the 7.10pm from Aberdeen, the southbound Aberdonian. The northbound Tynesider passed through, nearing its journey's end, at around 5.10am and, finally, on Fridays, The Continental, the once-a-week Dover-Newcastle car sleeper at around 7am.

The first titled daytime train was The North Briton, the 9.15am from Leeds City to Glasgow via York at about 10.15am and then, within minutes of each other, came the 9.20am Newcastle-King's Cross - the Up Tees-Tyne Pullman and, if it was a Wednesday or a Thursday, The Norseman, the 8.40am from Tyne Commission Quay to King's Cross. The morning Up Talisman, the 7.30am Edinburgh-King's Cross would come racing through at about 10.45 and at around 11.15 the Up Northumbrian, the 10.5am from Newcastle. Minutes later the northbound Talisman, the 7.45am from London, would storm through in the opposite direction. From lunchtime came a parade of named expresses which included the most famous of all. The southbound Elizabethan, non-stop from Edinburgh(dep 9.45am) to London with its corridor tender A4 Pacific at the head would scorch through at around 12.45pm

and its northbound counterpart about 20 minutes later followed soon after, on Mondays, Wednesdays and Thursdays, by the northbound Norseman. Ten minutes after that the 10am Edinburgh-King's Cross, the Flying Scotsman, would be flying past and, if it was a Monday, an Up working of The Norseman followed. Then, at about 1.45pm, came the 10am King's Cross-Edinburgh - the northbound Flying Scotsman. At approximately 3.25pm the southbound Queen of Scots - the 11am Pullman from Glasgow eased gracefully through on its way to King's Cross - one of the few expresses to slow down for Northallerton as it took the junction for Harrogate and Leeds. The observer then had just over an hour to catch their breath and have a cup of tea before the northbound Queen of Scots at about 4.35 and the 12.20pm Northumbrian from King's Cross at about 4.50. The southbound Heart of Midlothian passed through at about 5.35, the last of the afternoon named expresses. Evening kicked off at around 6.20 with the northbound Heart of Midlothian, the 2pm King's Cross-Edinburgh, and then the southbound afternoon Talisman at about 7.15, its northbound counterpart storming through around 20 minutes later. The returning Tees-Tyne Pullman would pass at around 8.35pm and finally, some 20 minutes later, the returning North

Briton. If a Wednesday, The Continental, the 8.45pm, Newcastle-Dover car sleeper rolled through and, if a Friday, The Highlands, the 9.55pm York-Inverness car sleeper, which returned in the early hours of Sunday morning. What a feast!

Other named expresses to pass through Northallerton during this era included the King's Cross-Perth Fair Maid which ran only between autumn 1957 and autumn 1958 in place of the morning Talisman, and, from 1960, the Holloway-Edinburgh and return Anglo-Scottish Car Carrier, always an impressive sight with its name emblazoned on the sides of its red car carrier vans.

In 1962 the government appointed Dr. Richard Beeching, a sharp-minded executive from ICI on nearby Teesside, as chairman of the then British Transport Commission with the task of cutting BR's mounting financial losses and dragging it out of the steam age. There would be no place for romanticism or tradition and very soon the famous named expresses began to disappear along with the famous steam locos that pulled them. Instead, they would all come under the highly successful Inter-City brand. BR became more interested in the premium-fare business travel market and by the end of the decade had introduced its fast Deltic-hauled "Executive" trains running to London in the early morning and back in the evening to give business travellers a full day in the capital. By 1973 the only remaining named expresses on the York-Darlington stretch were the North Briton, The Talisman, The Tees-Tyne Pullman, a daytime Aberdonian and The Flying Scotsman along with the Night Aberdonian, The Night Scotsman and The Night Capitals sleeper trains. The car sleeper services now came under the generic Motorail brand.

Passengers travelling to London from Northallerton or Thirsk were not privy to any of the ECML's prestigious trains in any case but in summer 1957, for instance, Northallerton did at least have one daily morning express to London in the shape of the 7am Newcastle-King's Cross via Sunderland departing at 9.13 and reaching London four and a half hours later. For a return service, however, they had to make do with a King's Cross-Sunderland through carriage on the 7.1pm York to Newcastle which also took four and a half hours - except on Fridays when there was a through train, the 3pm King's Cross-Newcastle which reached Northallerton at 7.13pm. The one other daily London train to call there was the 7.25pm from Newcastle, departing at 8.48pm. Mostly, however, they had to endure rather extended journeys by using local trains and changing at York.

Only a tiny proportion of passenger trains actually called at Northallerton, just 15 Down(northbound) and 16 Up(southbound) each weekday in summer 1957 plus the odd train which called there on a Monday or a Friday. The most important trains were the Liverpool Lime Street-Newcastle expresses, which departed at 12.26, 5.46 and 8.54pm to Newcastle, and to Liverpool at 10.7am via Ripon, 11.36am via York - and 6.21pm to Liverpool Exchange, also via York. One other, the 10.30am from Liverpool Exchange called at Thirsk but not Northallerton as it took the low level line to run via the Durham coast. The only other long distance expresses to call there daily were a Cardiff-Newcastle express at 3.39pm, and the 7.5pm Newcastle-Bristol, at 8.38pm.

Northallerton's remaining services were made up of the Leeds-York-Newcastle trains(three northbound - one starting from Bradford - and two southbound,) two morning York-Edinburgh trains which were more in the way of extended stopping services, two Newcastle-York trains, two Darlington-York locals(one continuing to Doncaster,) one York-Darlington,

In the mid-1950s A3 Pacific No. 60078 *Night Hawk* **storms past Thirsk with what appears to be the evening Newcastle-Bristol, one of the few long-distance trains to call at Northallerton.** *Neville Stead collection*

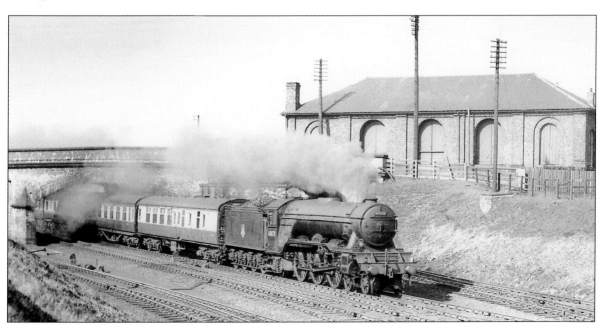

the 9.41pm York-West Hartlepool, departing Northallerton at 10.27, the 1.25pm Newcastle-Colchester at 1.53pm and the 3.50am York-Stockton - basically a newspaper and parcels train with passenger accommodation which departed Northallerton at 4.47. Three local trains arrived from Leeds via Ripon, one going forward to Middlesbrough, two left for Leeds via Ripon(one starting from Darlington) and one for Harrogate. Besides these were the Mondays Only 8.5am Darlington-King's Cross, a peak summer Bristol to Newcastle at 2.59pm, and a Fridays Only 6.52pm Newcastle-Birmingham, the latter pair running for only for a few weeks in high summer. But for a small number of exceptions and those trains running direct between Northallerton and Ripon, Thirsk had much the same level of service.

The service to smaller stations between Thirsk and York was by summer 1957 rudimentary to say the least, especially with the York-Pickering trains gone. Just one train in each direction served all stations, one each way served only Alne, and one Down train served only Pilmoor. Closure of all but Tollerton would soon follow.

After the 1960s Beeching cutbacks, Northallerton's service was, by summer 1968, even more spartan, especially with the loss of the Ripon service in 1967 and many Stockton line trains. The number of passenger trains calling there had slumped to just 11 each way. The only London service was the 07.45 from Sunderland leaving Northallerton at 09.02, which had so far survived the Beeching era. The few other long-distance trains to call there were the 12.00 Newcastle-Colchester(dep. 13.43,) 23.31 Edinburgh-Colchester(dep. 03.15,) and 08.05

Colchester-Newcastle(arr Northallerton 14.04,) the 07.35 Birmingham-Newcastle(arr. Northallerton at 11.00,) the 07.20 York-Aberdeen at 07.54, and the 19.10 Newcastle-Bristol mail at 20.36. The number of Newcastle-Liverpools calling there had been cut to just two northbound and one southbound while there were two Leeds-Newcastle diesel multiple units each way(one of the northbound trains running via Stockton.) The remaining services consisted of three York-Darlington DMUs each way(one extended to Newcastle and one to Leeds,) one other Newcastle-York train, one DMU from Darlington to Northallerton and two from Northallerton to Hartlepool, one going forward to Newcastle. The 03.50(now 03.40) from York still ran, but as a 75mph class 1 news and parcels train to Stockton and class 3 from there to Sunderland.

More cuts followed and by the start of the May 1973-74 timetable Northallerton was served by only ten daily trains each way on Mondays to Fridays. The 07.41 from Sunderland now ran only to York, the London service replaced by the 07.05 Darlington-King's Cross which left Northallerton at 07.20 and Thirsk at 07.30 to reach the capital at 11.10. The 17.23 Newcastle-King's Cross called at Northallerton at 18.27 and Thirsk at 18.38. The 18.30 King's Cross-Newcastle provided a return service from London, reaching Thirsk at 22.07 and Northallerton at 22.19. Just one Liverpool-Newcastle now served Northallerton, the 15.10 from Lime Street which called there at 18.11 while Northallerton and Thirsk's only other remaining long-distance services were the 07.15 York-Aberdeen and the 19.30 Newcastle-Bristol mail. The remainder of the two stations' service was provided by three York-Darlington

Trains between Pickering and York formed the backbone of the service for the small stations at the south end of the York-Northallerton main line until they were withdrawn in February 1953. After that, these stations were left with what amounted to a nominal service only and closure soon followed. Here, D20 No. 62345 comes round the curve from Sunbeck Junction to Bishophouse Junction with an early 1950s Pickering to York service. *J.W. Hague/Neville Stead collection*

locals each way, two Down and one Up York-Newcastle, a Leeds-Newcastle and a Darlington-Leeds, the 11.15 Leeds-Stockton, the 07.06 Hartlepool-York and the 13.18 Stockton-York. Apart from the Mondays Only 00.10 Darlington-King's Cross which stopped at Northallerton and Thirsk to set down passengers only, that was it.

The 1974 local government reorganisation created the county of North Yorkshire with Northallerton its administrative centre prompting calls for improved services but they must have fallen on deaf ears at BR because Northallerton and Thirsk saw little or no benefit from the new 125mph timetable introduced on 8th May1978. It showed just nine Up trains and ten Down trains calling there Monday to Friday, most of them York-Darlington DMUs. The only variations from these being the 07.41 Sunderland-York, 17.12 Darlington-Leeds, the 19.30 Newcastle-Bristol mail, the 07.06 York-Newcastle, 07.48 Leeds-Newcastle and the 15.10 Liverpool-Newcastle. The two stations now had no direct London service - the overnight Mondays Only Darlington-King's Cross still called there to set down. Saturdays were a different matter, with most local trains not running and the service instead comprising mainly Liverpool-Newcastle, Newcastle-South Wales and Birmingham-Newcastle trains as well as the 06.12 Newcastle-King's Cross, 17.55 Edinburgh-Leeds, and the 19.00 King's Cross-Newcastle. By this time the 07.41 Sunderland-York(to Scarborough on summer Saturdays) and the summer Saturday 07.15 Newcastle-Scarborough and 11.50 return were the only Stockton line trains calling Northallerton.

With the 1980s came a new enterprising style of BR management. Not only did more trains start serving Northallerton and Thirsk but there were more direct London trains including a named express which called at Northallerton. In the May 1983-May 1984 timetable, Northallerton's service had recovered to 13 Up and 10 Down trains and among them was The Cleveland Executive HST, introduced in 1981. The Up train, which started out from Sunderland at 05.49 left Northallerton at 07.21, the return, the 16.37 from King's Cross reaching Northallerton at 19.10. It provided what BR described as a Pullman-style at seat service in first class. Other London trains at the time were the 06.30 Newcastle-King's Cross, 17.55 Newcastle-King's Cross and 20.00 King's Cross-Newcastle HSTs. The remaining trains were a mixture of Liverpool-Newcastles which had been restored to three Down and four Up, a couple of Darlington-York DMUs each way, the 07.06 York-Newcastle, the 08.40 York-Aberdeen and 16.30 return(arrive 22.30,) the 08.10 Newcastle-Plymouth HST(Penzance on summer Saturdays,) the 13.28 Paignton-Newcastle HST(arrive 20.10,) and the overnight Darlington-King's Cross still stopping to set down only but now running every night and starting from Durham. All trains except The Cleveland Executive also called at Thirsk. The only additional summer Saturday train calling at Northallerton was the 13.30 Filey-Newcastle.

The following ten years saw more notable developments, including electrification of the ECML and the replacement of loco-hauled stock on the Newcastle-Liverpools with 90mph Class 158 DMUs. Although the Sunderland-King's Cross service was again consigned to history in October 1990, its name

dropped since May, its place so far as Northallerton was concerned, was taken by no less-a-train than the Tees-Tyne Pullman which called there at 07.02 from the start of what was the last all-diesel timetable on the ECML north of Doncaster. The northbound Pullman did not call at Northallerton but by this time the town was better served with London trains, the 14.30 and 16.30 King's Cross-Newcastle and 18.30 King's Cross-Edinburgh calling there along with the 09.35 Newcastle and 12.00 Edinburgh-King's Cross. More Newcastle-Liverpool trains were serving Northallerton again while the local service included two trains from Newcastle to Hull.

But the transformation in services could never be more dramatic than in May 1992 when BR introduced a new, mainly two-hourly, TransPennine service between Middlesbrough and Liverpool(odd ones to/from York)which set the pattern for the service level enjoyed in 2010. With the Newcastle-Liverpools these trains provided the backbone of the Northallerton and Thirsk service. But that was not all, Northallerton was also served by four direct trains to King's Cross - including the Tees-Tyne Pullman - and four from King's Cross. The total number of trains serving Northallerton each weekday had leapt to 21 Up and 20 Down. One stalwart which was no more, however, was the overnight London service stopping only to set down.

In the second half of the 1990s, private companies took over the running of Britain's railway network from BR with King's Cross expresses operated by Great North Eastern Railway - bringing the GNER initials back to the York-Darlington main line after 150 years. In 2007 GNER handed back the East Coast franchise, unable to meet the huge premium payments demanded by the government and National Express took over only to do the same in autumn 2009. At the time of going to press, ECML services were back in public ownership, operated by a government company called Directly Operated Railways, trading as East Coast. Other operators on this section of the ECML were Virgin CrossCountry which took over the North East-South West and South Coast services(since replaced by Arriva CrossCountry) and First TransPennine Express operating the Middlesbrough and Newcastle-Manchester services.

Improvements continued and in summer 2009, Northallerton enjoyed a level of service unimaginable back in the 1950s, the 1960s or even the 1970s - no less than 38 southbound trains and 37 northbound calling there. They consisted mainly of hourly Newcastle-Manchester Airport and Middlesbrough-Manchester Airport services operated by 100mph Class 185 DMUs, while there were no less than six East Coast expresses to King's Cross and back. Most remarkable of all has to be the arrival of independent operator Grand Central which reintroduced the Sunderland-King's Cross service using its distinctive black HSTs, not just one train a day but three each way(increased to four in December) and all calling at Thirsk as well as Northallerton. With them came American-style names, the 06.41 from Sunderland being The Zephyr and the 16.50 return service from King's Cross The 21st Century Limited. Meanwhile the only East Coast named trains to be seen on the York-Darlington main line in 2009 were The Flying Scotsman - who would dare abolish that one -The Northern Lights between King's Cross and Aberdeen and The Highland Chieftain between King's Cross and Inverness.

The Leeds Northern route through Ripon was regarded as an important main line but passenger traffic was relatively light. Its most prestigious train was The Queen of Scots, which in summer 1960 passed Ripon at 3.37pm southbound and 4.14pm northbound(4.19 on Saturdays.) It did not stop anywhere between Harrogate and Darlington but Ripon had its own London train - the 10.38am to King's Cross(10.56 on Saturdays) and the 10.20am(10.52 on Saturdays) from King's Cross which terminated at Ripon at 3.28pm(3.54 on Saturdays.)

In summer 1957, the advertised Monday to Friday passenger service through Ripon consisted of 11 trains each way. Apart from The Queen of Scots and the Ripon-King's Cross, the most important trains were those on the Newcastle-Liverpool route consisting of the 8.55am from Newcastle(departing Ripon at 10.27,) the 4.13pm from Newcastle(from Ripon at 6.17,) the 9am from Liverpool(arrive Ripon 12.2pm) and the 2.20pm from Liverpool(arrive Ripon 5.23.) Supplementing these were the Mondays, Fridays and Saturdays Only 10am Sunderland-Manchester Exchange which ran daily in high summer, the Fridays Only 4.10pm Sunderland-Liverpool, the Mondays, Fridays and Saturdays Only 9.30am Manchester Exchange-Newcastle, and on Saturdays the 5.37pm Manchester Exchange-Newcastle.

The remaining daily trains were local services which ran mainly between Leeds, Harrogate, Thirsk, Northallerton, Darlington, Middlesbrough, and West Hartlepool as well as the 7.35pm from Bradford Exchange which terminated at Ripon at

8.58pm to be the last Monday-Friday arrival of the day from Leeds. Later trains ran on Saturdays, being the 8.45pm Harrogate-Darlington and the 10.30pm Harrogate-Thirsk. The last train of the day southbound was the 8.40pm Northallerton-Leeds which left Ripon at 9.10pm. First trains were the 3.52am from Leeds which terminated at Ripon at 5.3 followed by the 5.50 Leeds-Thirsk(dep. Ripon 7am,) and the 7.8am Northallerton-Leeds departing Ripon at 7.35am.

Four northbound and three southbound Monday-Friday trains ran via the Thirsk-Melmerby line along with the 8.45pm and 10.30pm Saturdays Only trains from Harrogate.

The line through Ripon was somewhat busier on Saturdays in the summer, mainly with extra trains ferrying holidaymakers between the North East and west coast resorts. They included the 10.7am West Hartlepool-Blackpool via Ilkley with portions from Saltburn and to Southport and departing Ripon at 11.22, and its return working which did not stop at Ripon but passed through at around 4.45pm. There was also the 11.20am Newcastle-Llandudno which did not stop and the 9.15am return which called at Ripon 2.20-23pm, and the 9.35am Leeds-Saltburn(10.27 from Ripon,) and 10.40am return which did not stop. An additional 12.50pm Northallerton-Leeds via Thirsk ran instead of the 12.45 Northallerton-Harrogate along with the additional 9.6am Leeds-Newcastle which did not stop at Ripon, and the 2.5pm Liverpool-Newcastle which called at Ripon 5.10-5.12. Extra trains also ran for Ripon races.

By summer 1960, two significant events had effected Leeds Northern services. One was the replacement of steam with DMUs on most local services, the other was closure of the Melmerby-Thirsk line which took place with effect from 14th

A typical 1950s pre-diesel local service on the Leeds Northern. D49/2 "Hunt" class 4-4-0 No. 62727 *The Quorn* of 50D Starbeck shed restarts a northbound stopping passenger train from Ripon station. *J.W. Hague/Neville Stead collection*

Immaculately turned-out A3 No. 60077 *The White Knight,* **from Newcastle's Heaton shed, passes Ripon signal box and approaches the station with what is almost certainly a Newcastle-Liverpool express in the late 1950s.** *J.W. Hague/Neville Stead collection*

September 1959 although the advertised Monday-Friday service through Ripon remained little changed with 12 northbound trains and 11 southbound. One minor change was that the Saturday Only 10.30pm from Harrogate now ran to Melmerby instead of Thirsk. The 1960 working timetable, however, reveals some interesting workings, such as the Sundays Only 11.15pm Leeds-Ripon DMU which continued unadvertised to Northallerton, returning as the unadvertised Mondays Only 12.50am Northallerton-Harrogate which called at Ripon 1.12-1.15am, and the 5.23am Melmerby to Harrogate(5.13 Ripon-Starbeck on Mondays Only) empty stock off the 3.57am Leeds-Ripon which had presumably run empty to Melmerby for the engine to run round. The summer Saturday 9.47am Newcastle to Manchester Exchange stopped at Ripon 11.42-47 but only for the engine to take water, and there was a mystery daily light engine from Harrogate(from Starbeck shed prior to its closure) booked to arrive Ripon at 6pm - presumably to assist the 4.13pm Newcastle-Liverpool which stood at Ripon from 6.14 to 6.19. Two other unadvertised passenger services in the WTT were the summer Saturday 5.20am Leicester London Road to Craigendoran booked past Ripon at 9.56am and the 1pm return past Ripon at 6.51pm. There was a Sunday service but it was sparse and consisted mainly of local trains.

Decline set in during the 1960s and no more so then at the end of the winter 1963/64 timetable when the Queen of Scots ceased running north of Leeds - but continued to run between Leeds and King's Cross, having taken over the name of the White Rose. All passenger services were then withdrawn from

the Harrogate-Northallerton section on 6th March 1967, the Liverpool-Newcastle trains being rerouted via York, the remaining two stations at Ripon and Melmerby closed to passengers, and the line closed to all traffic between Melmerby and Northallerton.

Nowadays the Leeds Northern line north of Northallerton carries frequent and regular express passenger services as outlined earlier but it has not always been so. At one time, it carried a mixture of trains travelling via York and Ripon. On Mondays to Fridays in summer 1950 a dozen advertised daily trains used the route northbound and 10 southbound. North of Picton, they were augmented by Stockton-Whitby trains until they were withdrawn in June 1954. The most important weekday trains were the 7.40am Mondays, Fridays and Saturdays Only West Hartlepool-King's Cross conveying through carriages from Saltburn, the 7.50am Sunderland-King's Cross, the 12.15pm Newcastle-York buffet car express, the 9.55am and 4.15pm Newcastle-Liverpool Lime Street, the Fridays Only 10.10pm South Shields to King's Cross, the 10.55pm Sunderland-King's Cross sleeper, the 9.43am Mondays, Fridays and Saturdays Only Manchester Exchange-Newcastle, the 10.20am Bristol-Newcastle, and the 10.25am Liverpool Exchange-Newcastle. Making up the backbone of the line's service were the 3.55am and 9.35pm York-West Hartlepool, 7.25am Leeds-West Hartlepool, 9.17am Leeds-Middlesbrough, 11.35am and 5pm Leeds-Newcastle, the 7.25am Sunderland-York, and the Mondays, Fridays and Saturdays Only 9.35am(also 3.55pm Fridays Only)South Shields-Manchester Exchange. Several local trains started and ended their journeys at Northallerton.

Northallerton's D20 4-4-0 No. 62347 departs Picton with a southbound local service in the early 1950s. The photographer was standing on the horse dock with the goods shed behind him. *Armstrong Railway Photographic Trust*

These were the 7.20am and 5.11pm to West Hartlepool, 3.40pm to Stockton, the 12.55pm from Middlesbrough arriving at 1.53, and the 5.53pm and 6.45pm from West Hartlepool which pulled into Northallerton at 7.3 and 8.13pm respectively. These trains together with the 9.17 Leeds-Middlesbrough served the intermediate stations at Brompton, Welbury and Picton but Welbury, just over five miles north of Northallerton, closed in 1954.

Ten years later the summer 1960 working timetable showed the route carrying just seven regular weekday trains northbound but 11 southbound with some noticeable changes which had taken place during the 1950s. The Sunderland-King's Cross still ran but it now included a portion from Saltburn, and there was a separate 7.5am Saltburn-King's Cross and 2pm return - named The Tees-Thames. Other principal trains to pass this way included the 12.5pm Newcastle-Colchester, 4.13pm Newcastle-Liverpool Lime Street, the 10.25pm Newcastle-King's Cross sleeper, 10.30am Liverpool Exchange-Newcastle and the 10.30am Bristol-Newcastle. Some trains ran only on certain days, such as the high summer Tuesdays and Thursdays Only 7.32am Sunderland-King's Cross, the Mondays, Fridays and Saturdays Only 10am Sunderland-Manchester Exchange(also to Leeds on Tuesdays and Thursdays in high summer,) the Fridays Only 4.8pm Sunderland-Liverpool Exchange, the Fridays Only 9.40pm Newcastle-Bournemouth, the Mondays, Fridays and Saturdays Only 9.30am Manchester Exchange-Newcastle, the Fridays Only 8.15am Swansea-Newcastle, the Fridays and Saturdays Only 5.38pm Manchester

Exchange-Newcastle, and the Fridays Only 2.50pm(Saturdays 3.5) King's Cross-Newcastle which started from York at 6.47 Tuesday to Thursday.

Other services at this time were the 6.50am Middlesbrough-York, the Mondays Only 7.32am Saltburn-York, 11.20am Middlesbrough-Harrogate, 6.12pm Sunderland-York, 3.50am York-Stockton, 7.52am Leeds-Middlesbrough, 11.40am Leeds-Newcastle, and the 9.25pm(9.50 on Saturdays) York-West Hartlepool - all but the 3.50am from York being DMUs.

That same summer there were enough Saturday extras to more than double the number of passenger trains on this section of the Leeds Northern. Following one after the other, passing Northallerton between 9.2 and 11.22am, were the 7.36am Sunderland-Bristol, the 8.40am Saltburn-King's Cross, the 8.53am Sunderland-Yarmouth, the 9.4am Sunderland/9.5 Saltburn-King's Cross, the 9.40am Saltburn/10.7 West Hartlepool-Blackpool, the 9.20am South Shields/9.50 Saltburn-King's Cross, and the 9.38am South Shields-Manchester Exchange. In the opposite direction during this period were the 9.40am Leeds City-Saltburn and the 8.55am Filey Holiday Camp-Newcastle. The 10.26am Newcastle-Filey Holiday Camp then passed Northallerton at 12.9pm and at 12.39pm the 10.50am Scarborough-Newcastle which was followed at 1.25 by the 10am Liverpool Exchange-Newcastle. After a lull, came the afternoon rush of trains carrying holidaymakers returning home to the North East. First, booked to pass, at 2.53pm was the 8.40am Bristol-Newcastle, then at 4.29 the 8.5am Bournemouth-Newcastle, at 5pm the 1.5pm Blackpool Central-

West Hartlepool and Saltburn, and at 5.32 the 10.10am Yarmouth-Newcastle. Saturday nights saw the 8.30pm Newcastle-Paignton booked to pass Northallerton at 10.15 and the 9.8pm Newcastle-Exeter car sleeper at 10.41. As was often the case with trains not booked to stop at Northallerton, many passed below the station on the low level lines via Boroughbridge Road.

Inevitably, the retrenchment of the 1960s brought a major reduction in the number of passenger trains using Northallerton-Eaglescliffe section of the Leeds Northern. The May 1968-May 1969 working timetable shows just four regular weekday passenger trains remaining northbound plus three summer Saturday extras, and five regular southbound services with the 10.40 Newcastle-Filey Holiday Camp the only summer Saturday extra. The Tees-Thames was long-gone, having ceased running in autumn 1961. Those regular services which survived were, with Northallerton times: 07.45 Sunderland-King's Cross(09.00,) the 09.20 Northallerton-Hartlepool DMU, 09.50 Newcastle-Liverpool(dep.11.30,) 11.52 Leeds-Newcastle DMU(dep.13.11,) 12.00 Newcastle-Colchester(pass 13.42,) 18.21 Northallerton-Newcastle DMU,18.27 Sunderland-Northallerton DMU(arr 19.50,) 17.05 King's Cross-Newcastle(pass 21.06) and the 22.20 Newcastle-King's Cross sleeper(pass 00.15.) The 03.50 York-Stockton had become the 03.40 York-Sunderland class 3 parcels. The three Down summer Saturday extras were the 09.30 Manchester Exchange-Newcastle, the 10.10 Filey Holiday Camp-Newcastle and the

06.30 Plymouth-Newcastle. Sundays saw five Up daytime-trains including two from Newcastle to King's Cross and two Newcastle-Liverpools(one going only to Manchester Victoria in high summer,) plus a Newcastle-Doncaster but the only booked Down trains were the 03.50 and 19.20 York to Newcastle.

With the new timetable on 4th May 1970 a new London service via the coast and Stockton was introduced - and a named train at that - when BR made a slight diversification away from the high-fare business traveller market in a bid to compete with newly introduced Newcastle-London express coaches. The train was The Highwayman which, despite being a slow, meandering service composed of mark 1 coaches, Gresley buffet car and Class 40 locomotive, did not stop at Northallerton or Thirsk. It was identifiable by the crossed gold pistols on its carriage window labels as it passed by on its way between Newcastle and Finsbury Park - which was as near to King's Cross as it was allowed to get. On Mondays to Fridays the Up train left Newcastle at 09.15 while the Down train was due to pass Northallerton at around 13.35; both Up and Down trains ran much later in the day on Saturdays.

Three years later there were even less passenger trains. The only Down local service in the May 1973-May 1974 timetable was the 11.15 Leeds-Stockton, departing Northallerton at 12.38 and the only Up local services the 07.20 Newcastle-York and 13.18 Stockton-York. Besides these the 01.15 King's Cross-Newcastle, 22.20 Newcastle-King's Cross sleeper and

D20 No. 62359, also of Northallerton shed, arrives at Northallerton with a 1950s stopping service from West Hartlepool in 1953.
J.W. Hague/Neville Stead collection

on Friday nights from June to September the 21.20 Newcastle-Newquay also travelled this way. The 09.29 Bridlington-Newcastle, 11.15 Newcastle-Filey Holiday Camp and 10.05 Newquay-Newcastle(calling Northallerton at 19.53) were the only summer Saturday extras. The 00.30 King's Cross-Newcastle, the 03.50 and 19.06 York-Newcastle, the summer service 10.30 Newcastle-King's Cross,13.40 Newcastle-King's Cross,18.35 Newcastle-Doncaster and the Newcastle-King's Cross sleeper were the only regular passenger trains between Eaglescliffe & Northallerton on Sundays.

By May 1978 the Northallerton-Eaglescliffe section had all but become a freight only line with just one advertised daily passenger train, the 07.15 Newcastle-York(08.57 from Northallerton) which continued to Scarborough on summer Saturdays. The only others were the summer Friday night Newcastle-Newquay, the summer Saturday 11.50 Scarborough-Newcastle and 10.00 Newquay-Newcastle, the Newcastle-King's Cross sleeper by now running from Eaglescliffe to Darlington. No passenger trains ran this way on Sundays unless diverted from the ECML because of engineering work. From 1981, as recounted earlier, The Cleveland Executive began running, starting a revival of passenger services on the route and such is the change in fortunes that in 2010 there may well be more passenger trains than freight on the line.

For a century the mainly single line from Northallerton to Hawes was Wensleydale's main artery with passengers using the service for work, business, market, shopping, school and leisure, patronage boosted by such tourist attractions as Aysgarth Falls, Castle Bolton and Jervaulx Abbey. Passenger trains were often of a mixed nature conveying milk and other perishables such as cheese and eggs along with vans for cattle and sheep - and racehorses for Middleham stables, BR road horse boxes being provided at Leyburn for the short journey to and from Middleham. Milk tankers were attached to passenger trains at Leyburn where the Express Dairy had a siding and were transferred to main line trains at Northallerton for movement further afield. Churns were picked up at intermediate stations and moved in special vans to Northallerton where in 1905 the NER had built a dairy on the Down side, north of the station, which it let to the Wensleydale Pure Milk Society, a local farmer's co-operative. The society also had its own six-wheeled milk van attached to Wensleydale trains. The dairy was ultimately sold to Cow & Gate and continues in business in 2010 though without rail traffic. A rail trolley, pushed by two men walking on the track was used to transport cream from the dairy to the station where it was despatched by passenger train. The dairy sent vans every day to destinations in the North East, the West Riding and London. Milk also went via Garsdale to the Express Dairy at Appleby, on the Settle & Carlisle line. After peaking in the 1920s when there was a

A good deal of Wensleydale's milk output was carried in tank wagons attached to passenger trains at Leyburn, a job for which one of Northallerton's Sentinel vertical-boilered steam locos was outbased there. On 27th March 1954, Class Y3 No. 68182 is uncoupled from milk tanks it has just shunted onto a Northallerton-bound train. *Neville Stead collection*

An idyllic scene to be found in Wensleydale day in day out until 1954. Not too many passengers and G5 0-4-4T No. 67314 in charge of the westbound service as two trains pass at Aysgarth on 27th March 1954. *Neville Stead collection*

dedicated milk train from Hawes to York and two milk trains a day from Hawes to Garsdale, milk traffic gradually switched to road transport. Millions of gallons were still carried by rail in the 1930s but declined rapidly after the passenger service was withdrawn, although some tanks continued to run between Leyburn and Cricklewood, north London, until the 1960s.

In summer 1950 the branch as far west as Hawes carried five westbound and four eastbound trains on Mondays to Fridays. They consisted of the 7.15am Northallerton-Garsdale, 10.15am Garsdale-Northallerton, 4.10pm Northallerton-Garsdale, 6.40pm Garsdale-Northallerton and 9.15pm Northallerton-Leyburn; the 7.52am Leyburn-Northallerton, 9.30am Northallerton-Leyburn, 3pm Leyburn-Hawes and the 4pm Hawes-Northallerton. Besides these were the 3.16pm Garsdale-Hawes and 4.25 return. On Saturdays the 9.30am from Northallerton continued through to Garsdale, forming an additional 12.55pm back to Northallerton while the 3pm Leyburn-Hawes started from Northallerton at 2.3pm. Trains called at all stations except Spennithorne where some were booked to call, others not, and the 7.15am and 9.15pm from Northallerton when required to set down passengers. The 34-mile Northallerton-Hawes journey time took between an hour and a half and an hour and three quarters. The 5.75 miles between Garsdale and Hawes took between 11 and 14 minutes. A rudimentary Sunday service was provided by the 3.45pm Northallerton-Leyburn and 5.10pm return milk train conveying added passenger coaches.

The dale's scenic attractions made it a popular venue for excursions which came in from both the Northallerton and Garsdale ends. But not all specials came for just the scenery. Well documented are the events of June 1927 when a host of excursion trains brought hundreds of visitors to witness a total eclipse of the sun, Leyburn being on the line of totality. They came from as far away as London, Norwich, Colchester, Nottingham, Hull and Dewsbury and to oversee the operation a temporary control office was set up in a coach in Leyburn goods yard along with an old tender for refilling train water supplies and cylinder wagons for replenishing the gas. At the start of world war two over a thousand children were evacuated from Tyneside to Askrigg and Leyburn. In the 1970s BR in partnership with the Yorkshire Dales National Park ran a number of excursions from Newcastle, Leeds and York to Redmire, not just bringing visitors to the dale but some with return workings enabling local residents to have a day in town by train. In 1981 BR judged the operation uneconomic and the last one ran on 20th April.

Since the 1930s, more convenient buses had been creaming off the railway's passenger business until in 1953 British Railways stated that each train was carrying only a handful of people and that withdrawal of the service would save £14,500 a year - a princely sum then, of course. Regular passenger services between Northallerton and Hawes were therefore withdrawn with effect from 26th April 1954 leaving the line to freight and the occasional excursions, for which station platforms were retained. One train each way soldiered on between Garsdale and Hawes until it too was axed on 16th March 1959

Despite the withdrawal of regular passenger services in 1954 and progressive closures since, the Wensleydale line has continued to attract excursion traffic up to the present day. This DMU special seen entering Leyburn station on its return from Redmire to York was run on 16th September 1978 by British Rail and the Yorkshire Dales National Park Committee. The Wickham platelayers' trolley on the platform is No. DB965085. *Stephen Chapman*

when that section of the branch closed completely.

Passenger services to Masham were withdrawn as long ago as 1st January 1931. In 1922 the advertised service consisted of the 7am Masham-Ripon, 9.17 Ripon-Masham, 10.10 Masham-Ripon, 12.20pm Melmerby-Masham, 1pm Masham-Ripon, 5.5 Ripon-Masham, 5.50 Masham-Ripon and 7.25 Ripon-Masham. Trains were worked from Masham by a G5 0-4-4T outbased there from Starbeck. The Masham-Ripon journey took between 20 and 22 minutes for the 10.75 miles. Bradshaw's July 1922 Railway Guide advised passengers to alight at Masham for Hack Fall(3.5 miles away) and Swinton Park(1.5 miles away.)

The independent Easingwold Railway withdrew its passenger service on 29th November 1948. Back in 1922 this little 2.5-mile light railway enjoyed an impressive service of eight trains each way per day starting with the 7.36am from Easingwold and finishing with the 7.18pm from Alne. The journey took eight minutes. By summer 1946, however, the writing was on the wall with the service just two trains each way on weekdays: the 8.8am and 5pm from Easingwold and the 9.7am and 5.57pm from Alne. An additional 12.50pm from Easingwold and 1.10pm from Alne ran on Saturdays.

Other services not directly included in this edition of Railway Memories but coming into the area at Pilmoor were the York-Pickering trains and those on the Boroughbridge branch.

Three York-Pickering trains each way Monday to Saturday in summer 1950(see Railway Memories No.19) followed the ECML between York and Bishophouse Junction serving Beningbrough, Tollerton, Alne and Raskelf, while several trains between Glasgow, Newcastle and Scarborough also took the Malton line on summer Saturdays until 1962. Trains arrived at Pilmoor from Harrogate via Boroughbridge on weekdays in summer 1950 at 7.18am and 5.40pm and left Pilmoor at 8.6am and 6.16pm. Extra trains on Saturdays Only departed Pilmoor at 1.28 and 8.48pm and arrived at 12.48, 8.23 and 11.31pm. The Boroughbridge line passenger service was withdrawn at the end of the summer 1950 timetable and the Pilmoor end of the line severed. The York-Pickering service was axed on 2nd February 1953 and the York-facing Sunbeck curve taken out of use.

Traditionally, parcels, newspapers and mail were conveyed to and from local stations in vans attached to passenger trains but from the 1950s three events - one peculiar to this area - increased the need for dedicated parcels trains. One was the replacement of steam-hauled passenger trains with diesel multiple units which only had limited capacity for parcels, the growth in mail-order catalogue shopping was another, and also the withdrawal of the Wensleydale passenger service. The number of parcels, news, mail and empty stock trains through Northallerton in summer 1960 has been mentioned earlier. Locally, the issue of limited space on DMUs was dealt with by allowing them to haul one or two tailvans, the number of vans permitted depending on the power rating of the unit concerned. The May 1968-May 69 working timetable showed the 17.10 York-Darlington and 20.41 York-Newcastle DMUs as booked to convey such vans. The 1969 Sectional Appendix stated that one vehicle of 17 tons gross weight was permitted for units of both 300 and 600hp.

One of the biggest catalogue shopping firms was Brian Mills who had their own terminal at Sunderland. During the 1960s the 7.50pm Sunderland-York parcels became the 20.40 Brian Mills-King's Cross, limited to 45mph as far as York and booked to pass Northallerton at 22.30. The 19.13 Brian Mills to Leeds was another, booked to run via Newcastle and then the ECML, passing Northallerton at 23.31.

Two return parcels trains a day was provided between Northallerton and Leyburn for milk and other traffic following withdrawal of the Hawes passenger service. The summer 1955 working timetable showed the morning working booked to depart Northallerton at 7.15am, arrive Leyburn 8.25, depart 12.30pm(1pm on Saturdays,) arrive Northallerton at 1.20pm(1.50 on Saturdays.) The afternoon working was booked to leave Northallerton at 4.5pm, arrive Leyburn 4.50pm, depart 5.20 and arrive back in Northallerton at 6.5pm. They were booked to call at all stations except Crakehall and Finghall Lane when required in both directions. By summer 1960 the service had been reduced to just the morning train,7.35am from Northallerton and 1pm from Leyburn.

Freight traffic

On the main lines, freight traffic through the area consisted of three flows making Northallerton an important freight crossroads - the NER planned a major marshalling yard there but it did not materialise and most freight continued to pass through. Two flows were, as today, between York and Teesside with its steel and chemical plants, and on the York and Darlington section. The third was between the North East and the West Riding via the Leeds Northern.

Freight trains on the first and second flows were far too numerous to mention individually. The winter 1959/60 working timetable showed no less than 86 Up freights(45 from the Teesside direction) through Northallerton each 24 hours on weekdays and 78(38 towards Teesside) in the Down direction. Many were at night. The most important trains were the fast class C express freights fully fitted with continuous brake on all wagons. Most notable was the 3.5pm King's Cross-Niddrie(Edinburgh) "Scotch Goods," booked for top link express passenger power - often an A4 Pacific - and passing Northallerton at 9.2pm. Of almost similar stature was the 2.55am King's Cross to Niddrie, passing Northallerton at 9.3am. The corresponding southbound train, the 6.5pm Niddrie-King's Cross, an "Assured Arrival" service running to accelerated Class C timings, was booked to pass Northallerton at 10.17pm. Of even greater priority were the 1.45pm Aberdeen-King's Cross fish and the 10.12am and 8.40am(when required) Aberdeen-King's

One of Sir Vincent Raven's original B16 4-6-0s, No. 61456, storms northwards through Pilmoor at the head of a fully fitted express goods consisting mainly of containers. *J.W. Hague/Neville Stead collection*

Cross meat trains which the working timetable instructed: "Takes precedence over all trains except East Coast passenger trains." Other high status class C freights were the Newcastle Park Lane to Birmingham Washwood Heath "The Birmingham Braked" due past Northallerton at 8.20pm and the 6.50pm Hull to Glasgow, The "Humber-Clyde", a service with an "Assured Arrival" time running to accelerated class C timings as far as Croft Yard(Darlington) and passing Northallerton at 9.16pm. Class C expresses also came through Northallerton on their way from King's Cross to Newcastle Forth, Whitemoor to Niddrie and Newcastle New Bridge Street, Dagenham Dock to Niddrie, York Dringhouses to Newcastle New Bridge Street, Dringhouses to Newcastle Park Lane via Stockton, London Ferme Park and Dringhouses to Heaton, Ferme Park to Niddrie, King's Cross and Healey Mills to Newcastle Park Lane via West Hartlepool, Immingham to Consett, Neville Hill to Croft and Stockton via Ripon, Newcastle Park Lane to Hull, four trains every 24 hours from Stockton to Dringhouses and five trains conveying fertilizer from Stockton to Skelton sidings(York,) Niddrie to Dringhouses, Newcastle Forth to Whitemoor, Inverkiething to King's Cross, Park Lane to King's Cross, Newcastle Forth to Doncaster Decoy, Darlington to Neville Hill via Ripon, Darlington to Immingham, Newport to Dringhouses, Heaton to Dringhouses, Newcastle Forth to York Clifton, and one each from West Hartlepool, South Stockton, Middlesbrough Goods, Port Clarence, Wearmouth and Washington to Dringhouses. Besides these were the Tuesdays and Saturdays Only London Park Royal to Newcastle Argyle Street "intermodal" - actually conveying Guinness road tankers on flat trucks - which passed Northallerton at the unearthly hour of 3.32am and the returning empty tankers through at a more viewable 4.4pm on Tuesdays and Thursdays, while the Burton to Niddrie beer train swilled its way through Northallerton at 3.50am each Tuesday morning. One can ponder at length just how much ale flowed through Northallerton between 3.30 and 4am on a Tuesday morning! At the appropriate time of year, three class C trains ran each day carrying Scottish seed potatoes - mostly during the daytime - from Niddrie to Whitemoor for East Anglian farmers plus two from Niddrie to York for their Yorkshire counterparts(some doubtless being planted in fields alongside the main line they had just travelled along,) and three to Doncaster for Lincolnshire farmers.

Class D express freights(vacuum brake fitted and operating on not less than 90 per cent of wagons) also ran from Whitemoor to Niddrie, Healey Mills and Normanton to Heaton, York to Wearmouth, Whitemoor to Stockton, Whitemoor to Croft, York to Newcastle Forth(three a day plus two a day from York to Park Lane,) Heaton to Doncaster Decoy, and Darlington and Heaton to York. The bulk of trains, however, were made up of class E and F partially fitted and H unfitted trains making their way between the yards at Newport, Croft, Stockton and West Hartlepool and the various yards at York, Normanton, Mirfield, Healey Mills, Neville Hill, Hull and Doncaster Decoy where they were re-sorted for the next stage of their journey. A few travelled longer distances such as Woodford Halse and Dewsnap to Newport, Newport to Mottram, Toton to Newport, Newport to Shrewsbury, Stockton and Newport to Annesley, and Croft to Whitemoor. Notable among the slow freights were the long-distance Mansfield to Uphall class H due through Northallerton at 5.20am and the Joppa to Sherwood class E empties at 12.29pm. Two class H iron ore trains from Storefield to Newport were due to pass on the low level at 10.2 and 10.37am with class F returning empties to Clay Cross at 8.58pm and at 3.17pm to what the working timetable described just as "London Midland Region."

A handful of trains also plied between Northallerton, Yorkand the marshalling yards situated just north of Thirsk station. Besides being an exchange point for Thirsk Town and

A familiar engine in this part of the world, V2 2-6-2 No. 60809 *The Snapper, The East Yorkshire Regiment, The Duke of York's Own* **ambles casually through Beningbrough on its way to York with an unfitted Through Freight on 27th March 1963.** *Peter Rose*

Melmerby branch local traffic, they also remarshalled limestone and chalk traffic bound for the Teesside furnaces from quarries around Pickering, Thornton Dale and the Wolds. The 1959/60 working timetable showed the daily 7.50am class H from Malton via Gilling booked to reach Thirsk at 10.5am from where its load of stone was worked forward to Newport at 11.45. If there was no traffic, the engine and brake van still came from Malton. The return working, which doubled as the pick-up, was untimed and left in the afternoon when ready.

By the mid-1960s many of these origins and destinations had disappeared, replaced by the big new marshalling yards such as Tees, Tyne, Healey Mills and, in Scotland, Millerhill. By then traditional wagonload traffic was in decline while the traffic that remained was changing beyond recognition. Familiar mixed goods trains and long rambling trains of loose-coupled coal wagons were giving way to air braked trainloads of steel, coal, aggregates, petrochemicals and Freightliner containers - often carrying far greater tonnages then the old style trains. By summer 1989 the number of freights through Northallerton had dropped to around 47 northbound, of which 31 went towards Teesside, and 42 southbound, of which 27 came from the Teesside direction. In 2009 they were down to around 28 each way in total and would have been much less were it not for the growth in imported and opencast coal from Scotland and the North East to the Yorkshire and East Midlands power stations.

The popular image on the southern half of the Leeds Northern is of successive goods trains slogging along behind Q6 0-8-0s and WD 2-8-0s from Newport and Neville Hill sheds.

In fact, by 1959 there were very few booked freights along the route, most having been rerouted via York following quadrupling of the ECML south of Northallerton to eliminate double heading on the steeply-graded section south of Harrogate. The first freight of the day on the line, passing Ripon at 2.5am, was the 1.20am Mondays excepted Darlington to Neville Hill class C. It was followed by the 1.35 Mondays excepted Newport to Neville Hill class H which was booked to take water at Ripon from 3.13 to 3.21. Both ran on Sundays as well. Next, on Thursdays Only, was the 3.25am Haverton Hill to Skipton class F which spent from 5.10 to 5.34am at Ripon taking water and allowing the 5.23am Melmerby-Harrogate empty stock to pass. Then, booked to arrive at 6.31am was the 6 o'clock class H goods from Starbeck which terminated at Ripon. Between 9.24 and 9.32am the 7.30am Mondays Only Haverton Hill to Skipton class H paused at Ripon for water. The next goods on the line was an untimed class K morning pick-up from Newport Yard to Melmerby. The return working of the 7.20am Northallerton Low Gates to Newport(which shunted Welbury and Picton when required,) it shunted Brompton, Newby Wiske, Pickhill and Sinderby goods yards when required. It returned when ready to Low Gates via Cowton(between Northallerton and Darlington,) shunting Sinderby, Pickhill, Newby Wiske and Danby Wiske if required. On weekdays there was nothing else booked until the returning Ripon to Harrogate Goods class H was due to leave at 6.22pm(11.14am on Saturdays.) On Tuesdays and Saturdays the 12.50pm class H from Heysham Moss was due to arrive Ripon for water at

The Heysham Moss to Haverton Hill tanks was one of the freights still travelling via Ripon into the 1960s as it was routed via Skipton, Ilkley and Harrogate. WD 2-8-0 No. 90503 has charge of the train as it crosses the River Ure at Ripon. *J.W. Hague/Neville Stead colln.*

6.55pm and continue its journey to Haverton Hill at 7.3. The two remaining trains of the day were the 9.25pm Neville Hill to Croft class C booked past Ripon at 10.36 and the 9.45pm Neville Hill-Stockton class C at 10.56.

After the passenger service was axed, a goods trip continued running to Ripon, and to Melmerby for military traffic, until October 1969 when the line from Harrogate to Melmerby was abandoned, military traffic thereafter being dealt with at Thirsk.

Freight traffic in Wensleydale was purely local and the line was not used as a through route for cross-Pennine trains but the railway was no sleepy branch line. Besides its passenger trains were at least three freight trains each way a day 1951.

Two daily pick-ups, worked by Northallerton engines and men, brought livestock, cattle feed, fertilizer, farm machinery, coal and general provisions and took away non-perishable produce not taken by passenger or parcels train as well as livestock, and limestone from the line's four quarry sidings. The first was the 6am class K from Northallerton goods yard to Jervaulx, returning as the 7.50 Jervaulx to Croft Yard and ending its diagram as the 11am Darlington Up siding to Northallerton. It shunted at Ainderby, Scruton, Leeming Bar, Bedale, Cowton, Croft Spa and Danby Wiske as required.

Right behind that was the 8am stone train from Wensley to Newport Yard or Cargo Fleet depending on the load. The return of the 4.15am empties from Tees Works, it was worked by a Middlesbrough engine and men and had the instruction: "Attaches Newport traffic at Leyburn if not a full load from Wensley."

The third train was the 10am Northallerton Goods Yard to Hawes pick-up which shunted all stations and Harmby Quarry as required, booked to return from Hawes at 1.30pm. It also conveyed water cans between Redmire to Bolton Gate House.

By September 1956 the Wensley stone train was running in the afternoon and the Jervaulx pick-up had ceased to run

Much freight switched to the roads during the 1950s but new traffic came the railway's way, including fuel oil to a terminal at Bedale, while the movement of limestone from Redmire quarry was increasing. The railway held on to enough local freight to keep a pick-up running through the 1970s, by which time it was mainly delivering coal and oil, and collecting stone. It ceased to run in 1982 when the remaining active goods yards were closed.

By 1959 the daily goods was the only other booked train on the branch besides the parcels train which it followed out of Northallerton. The winter 1959/60 working timetable showed the class K working booked away from Low Gates at 7.45am and thereafter running untimed to Hawes and back, Hawes being the end of the line since March. On the outward run, it was booked to shunt when required at Finghall Lane, Constable Burton, Leyburn, Wensley, Redmire, Aysgarth and Askrigg, and on the return at Askrigg, Aysgarth, Redmire, Wensley, Leyburn, Harmby Quarry, Constable Burton, Finghall Lane, Bedale, Leeming Bar, and to detach wagons at Castle Hills siding before returning to Low Gates. Although they were listed in the WTT, no provision was shown for stops at Ainderby, Scruton, Jervaulx, Ord & Maddison's Quarry west of Leyburn, or at Crakehall and Spennithorne.

The pick-up ceased to run beyond Redmire in April 1964 and the line from there to Hawes was closed but the amount of stone being despatched from Redmire ensured the remaining

Wensleydale freight in steam days. K1 2-6-0 No. 62045 calls at Redmire with the pick-up. *J.W. Hague/Neville Stead collection*

Wensleydale freight in the 1990s. The crew of Class 60 No. 60038 *Bidean Nam Bian* and the Redmire-Tees limestone train exchange tokens with the signalman at Bedale on 26th April 1991. Little did anyone know that in less than a couple of years this, the Wensleydale line's only remaining train, would cease running and the branch would face total abandonment. *Stephen Chapman*

branch's survival to the present day. While output from the quarries at Harmby, Ord & Maddison's and Wensley was dwindling away, Redmire became the principal supplier of limestone for British Steel's Teesside works which had been completely rebuilt in the late 1970s. It warranted a block train running six days a week which in the summer 1989 working timetable was shown as train 6N53, the 09.25 from Redcar British Steel mineral terminal, arriving Redmire at 13.32 with slightly different times on Saturdays. On the return, it was booked to depart Redmire at 14.40, train 6N54, for Tees Yard which it reached at 17.45, having taken nearly two hours to travel from Redmire to Castle Hills due to the many level crossings which had to be operated by the train crew. In both directions, the train had to be propelled between Northallerton and Castle Hills Junction. The Wensleydale line's whole future came under threat in the early 1990s when British Steel judged the rail operation to be uneconomic and decided to switch to road transport. Following much opposition at the prospect of heavy lorries on Wensleydale roads, the company stuck with rail but changed its source to its own quarry at Shap. The Redmire train made its last run on 18th December 1992 and the line was mothballed pending possible preservation by the Wensleydale Railway Association. But no sooner had the stone traffic ceased than the Ministry of Defence, in the wake of a major review of its logistics operations, made a return to rail for long hauls of military equipment which included the transport of armoured vehicles to and from Redmire for use in exercises by nearby Catterick garrison. The first trial train ran in 1996 amidst a blaze of publicity and, despite one vehicle

slipping off a wagon at Redmire, was judged a success and the traffic has continued as required since.

The branch lines and local stations not so far mentioned were served by a network of local trips worked with locomotives and crews from York, Starbeck, Malton and Northallerton engine sheds. The York District Working of Local Freight and Mineral trains book issued on 19th September 1955 shows five trips operating in the area, all class K unless otherwise stated. York trip No.1 booked away from York Yard North daily for Thirsk Yard at 6.40am shunted Beningbrough, Tollerton, Alne, Raskelf, Pilmoor South and Sessay as required on the outward run and the same stations(Pilmoor instead of Pilmoor South,) on the return. It also delivered water cans as required. A special instruction stated "Alne and Easingwold traffic to be marshalled separately." Starbeck trip No.1 was booked to depart Starbeck daily for Otterington at 8.25am. It shunted when required at Ripon, Melmerby ordnance depot, Melmerby station, Baldersby, Topcliffe and Thirsk on both outward and return runs. It too delivered water cans where required while a special instruction stated that traffic for Nidd Bridge and Wormald Green(between Ripon and Harrogate) was to be detached at Melmerby on the outward journey. Starbeck trip No.3 worked the Masham branch starting from Ripon using the engine off the early morning freight from Starbeck. It also shunted at Ripon and later returned to Starbeck with the 6.27pm class H. Not running on Saturdays, the Masham goods was booked to leave Ripon at 1.6pm, shunting Melmerby and Tanfield as required on both outward and return trips. Malton trip No.2 to Thirsk Yard and back was the class H stone train doubling as

A truly idyllic scene if not a profitable one for the railway. J39 0-6-0 No. 64855 passes the peaceful village of West Tanfield as it ambles the daily pick-up towards Masham. *J.W. Hague/Neville Stead collection*

a pick-up shown in the WTT and referred to earlier but in 1955 there was also Malton trip No.5, an additional class H stone train which ran purely from Malton to Thirsk, and back with empties, on Mondays, Wednesdays and Fridays when traffic demanded. Northallerton shed provided an engine for shunting Thirsk Yard Monday to Saturday and working trips to Thirsk Town as required.

The Masham branch spent most of its life delivering provisions and coal to the local community and serving local agriculture except of course in the early 20th century when it also conveyed materials for construction of the Colsterdale resevoirs which were taken up into the valleys west of Masham by the narrow gauge railway mentioned earlier. The concentration of airforce bases throughout the area also generated traffic in fuel and munitions, especially during world war two when vast amounts of munitions were stored in the surrounding countryside. When the war ended, 17 special trains were needed to clear the remaining stocks. This town, which became famous for Theakston's Brewery, lost its railway when goods traffic ceased and the branch closed with effect from 11th November 1963 under a 1962 scheme to cut costs by concentrating freight traffic from a number stations in the area, including Pately Bridge and Boroughbridge, on Ripon. This left Wensleydale and Thirsk Town the only branches still in use. The decline in local goods traffic had a knock-on effect on local sorting yards with Thirsk closing during the late 1960s(references to Thirsk Yard were deleted from the Sectional Appendix per the 4-weekly notice issued on 7th June 1969.) In 2009 only a couple of sidings and a run-round loop remained, on the Down side, for engineers' or emergency use.

All change

Just as in the 19th century the railway revolution thrust society through a quantum leap in progress, so the 20th century saw the Great North of England main line of 1841 continue to evolve at the leading edge of technology while the remainder, having once spread across the landscape, retreated to leave the network we start the 21st century with.

In 1901 new lines were laid at the south end of Northallerton, one from Cordio Junction, on the Ripon line, to Northallerton station, and the other from Longlands Junction, on the Down side of the York line, to the low level Leeds Northern at Boroughbridge Road. The latter enabled freight trains from the York direction to reach Teesside and the Durham coast without making a conflicting movement across the main line at Northallerton station. The former allowed Ripon line passenger trains to reach Northallerton station. The Ripon line was doubled at the same time, becoming the main route for Leeds Northern expresses instead of that via Thirsk, and Northallerton Low station, the terminus of the local service from Melmerby, was closed and converted to a goods station. In 1904 the NER installed automatic semaphore signals between Alne and Thirsk, and before long was planning to electrify the York-Newcastle and Northallerton-Stockton lines. It built and tested a prototype express passenger locomotive but then came the 1923 Grouping when the NER was amalgamated with other companies such as the Great Northern, Great Central and North British to form the LNER which dropped the scheme.

Further developments came in the early 1930s when the LNER undertook a major upgrade of the York-Darlington main line. Extra running lines were laid at various points between Northallerton and York, electric colour light signalling and the first route relay interlocking system of its kind in the world were introduced and brought under the control of a handful of modernized signal boxes. A new cord was laid from Borough-bridge Road to the Up side at Longlands Junction, passing under the main line and allowing freight trains from Teeside and the Durham coast to avoid Northallerton station. The redundant overbridge which once carried the unused line connecting the Boroughbridge and Malton lines was removed to facilitate widening at Pilmoor. Further upgrading took place during the 1950s, including the installation of long welded rail in the Fast lines. By June 1960 the whole 30 miles between Northallerton and York was four-track - the last section completed being the Up Slow from Pilmoor to Alne. Overbridges were reconstructed to accommodate the wider lines and they were built with clearances for overhead wires in preparation for a second abortive electrification scheme. Signalling too was further modernized and brought under the control of power boxes at York, Skelton, Tollerton, Pilmoor, Thirsk and Northallerton. The 1960s saw work for 100mph running over what was traditionally one of the fastest stretches of railway in the country. Signalling around Thirsk was updated in 1964 and 14 route miles of quadruple track brought under the control of a modernized Thirsk signal box. The 1970s saw speeds further increased to 125mph for InterCity 125 High Speed Trains, and during a series of test runs with the prototype HST world speed records for diesel traction were set and broken between Northallerton and York every few days - or so it seemed.

The Leeds Northern north of Northallerton saw little more change than the progressive closure of all intermediate stations between Northallerton and its junction with the Stockton & Darlington line at Eaglescliffe, Brompton being the last to go on 6th September 1965. After that, little changed as the route settled into the routine of a trunk freight artery. But in 1997 signalling all the way from Northallerton to beyond Picton, and an interface with Bowesfield box on Teeside, was updated. brought under the control of Northallerton's Low Gates box and Track Circuit Block working introduced under one of Railtrack's "Efficiency by the Rationalisation of Signal Boxes" (EROS) schemes.The signal boxes at Long Lane(Welbury) and Picton were abolished as a result.

For the other lines, change meant little more than closure - and mostly before Dr. Beeching had even been heard of. The first took place as early as 1855, shortly after formation of the NER, when the new company closed Thirsk Town to passengers and rerouted all Leeds Northern services to the main line station. Even so, Thirsk Town stayed in business as a goods station for well over a century afterwards. As previously mentioned, the Masham branch lost its passenger service at the end of 1930, the Easingwold Railway in 1948, Pilmoor-Borough-bridge-Knaresborough in 1950, and Northallerton-Hawes in 1954. The Easingwold Railway closed completely on 30th December 1957 when goods and parcels traffic ceased, and Hawes-Garsdale in March 1959 upon the withdrawal of all traffic. Six months later, the original Leeds Northern main line from Melmerby to its junction with the Thirsk Town branch was

closed completely, having been relegated to a backwater ever since the Melmerby-Northallerton route was upgraded in 1901.

By the start of the 1960s, the only railways remaining in the area besides the ECML and Leeds Northern were Northallerton-Hawes, Melmerby-Masham, Thirsk Town(all goods only,) and the Pilmoor-Malton line. Then, in March 1963, a parcels train was derailed at Sessay Wood Junction and the track badly damaged. This was now the Beeching era and instead of the junction being repaired, the Malton line was simply closed and future summer Saturday trains rerouted via York. The Masham branch went completely on 11th November, the Wensleydale branch was cut back to Redmire on 27th April 1964, and Thirsk Town shut down in October 1966. The area's one true line closure under the Beeching plan occurred on 6th March 1967 when passenger trains between Harrogate and Northallerton were withdrawn or rerouted via York, and the Leeds Northern breached by total closure between Melmerby and Northallerton. The Harrogate-Melmerby section hung on for freight until October 1969 when that too was abandoned. Hope remains that one day the line will reopen between Harrogate and Ripon with feasibility studies having proved favourable, reporting that the £40 million cost of reopening would be recouped by an estimated 1,200 to 2,700 passengers a day even though some of the trackbed has been built on and some major structures demolished.

The last closure to take place, leaving the railway with the shape it has in 2010, occurred in 1970. The curve giving direct access from Northallerton station to the Wensleydale branch was deleted from the Sectional Appendix per the 4-weekly notice issued on 4th July.

Finally, an event which many began to think may never happen after two abortive schemes had bit the dust, occurred in 1984 when electrification of the entire East Coast main line to Edinburgh was authorized. It took seven years to complete during which it was described as Britain's biggest construction site. Again, cutting edge technology was introduced. Signalling between York and Danby Wiske where it interfaced with a similar establishment at Gateshead, was brought under the control of a computerized signalling centre at York(officially termed an integrated electronic control centre,) while a unique microwave telecommunications system which was state-of-the-art in the 1960s when it replaced the telegraph pole route, was itself replaced by the latest fibre-optic cables.

In 2000 the Wensleydale Railway Association formed the Wensleydale Railway Company which three years later took a 99-year lease on the 22-mile Redmire branch from Network Rail with the long term aim of reinstating the whole line through to Garsdale. Since 2004 it has run passenger trains between Leeming Bar and Redmire and plans to extend the operation to Northallerton station as soon as possible.

With the ECML, the northern half of the Leeds Northern, and the Wensleydale branch, Northallerton remains an important and busy junction if not a major railway centre - and visitors to Wensleydale can again enjoy its scenic delights from a train window as they roll gently by. As for the rest of the railway in this area, memories such as those in this book are about all we are left with.

Above: Crossing from the area covered by Railway Memories No.17 into the domain of Railway Memories No.23, A3 Pacific No. 60073 *St. Gatien* **collects water from Wiske Moor troughs as it heads an Up 1950s express.** *Ken Hoole/Neville Stead collection*

Left: A4 No. 60024 *Kingfisher* **being thrashed over Wiske Moor troughs when running 42 minutes late with the return leg of an A4 Locomotive Society Doncaster-Edinburgh special at 19.59 on 21st May 1966.** *Robert Anderson*

White and blue light beams were provided at Wiske Moor troughs to show firemen when to lower and raise their water scoops, lowering when passing through the white beam and raising when passing the blue beam.

The troughs were retained for a time after the end of express passenger steam to provide water for diesel locomotive train heating boilers. The 4-weekly notice dated 15th February 1969 stated: "English Electric 3300hp Deltic diesel electric locomotives. Until further notice the above locomotives must not exceed 70mph when taking up water at Wiske Moor Troughs in either direction."

At Wiske Moor Troughs a tramway left the Down side of the main line at right angles and ran for just over a quarter of a mile to a pumping station on the River Wiske which fed the troughs. Isolated from the main line, it is thought to have carried coal which must have been transhipped from wagons on a siding that was connected and fell out of use when the station was replaced by diesel pumps, though it was still shown on the 1962 Ordnance Survey map which also showed it to be standard gauge. What sort of propulsion was used, whether it was a horse or some other means, is unclear. The troughs themselves were renewed in 1952.

The October 1956 Darlington District working of local freight trains book showed Northallerton No.2 loco diagram booked to "Change water tenders to Danby Wiske" each fortnight.

Above: Class A2/2 Pacific No. 60501 *Cock o' the North* **rolls the southbound Queen of Scots past Northallerton signal box during the mid-1950s. Unlike most top link expresses, this one will be slowing down to take the right hand junction for the Ripon line. The power signal box and route relay interlocking signalling were commissioned on 3rd September 1939, the day war was declared on Germany. Its steep hipped, pagoda-like roof was characteristic of all the new boxes built between York and Darlington for the 1930s resignalling. It was abolished in 1990 when control was transferred to the new IECC at York.** *J.W. Hague/Neville Stead collection*

Below: The Queen of Scots 1960s-style. Deltic No. D9009 *Alycidon* **slows for the 25mph Ripon turn on a dismal 19th April 1963. Immediately right of the Deltic, in the the goods yard, is the canopy of the coal stage for Northallerton loco shed which itself was way down below on the low level line. The turntable was also here, beyond the coal stage. The chimney in the left background indicates the Cow & Gate dairy originally built by the NER and leased to the Wensleydale Milk Society.** *Rev. David Benson*

Above: Relegated to freight and shrouded in steam and murk, A3 No. 60091 *Captain Cuttle* forebodes the decline of steam as it eases a class 7 oil tank train through Northallerton station on 19th April 1963. The station goods yard on the right included coal drops and a cattle and goods dock. The 1956 Handbook of Stations described it as equipped for handling livestock, horse boxes and prize cattle vans, and carriages and motor cars by passenger or parcels train. There was no permanent crane. *Rev. David Benson*

Below: Another Pacific finding itself on lesser duties on 19th April 1963 was A4 No. 60005 *Sir Charles Newton*, forging northwards with an unfitted Through Freight. The station buildings and vehicle dock are on the left. *Rev. David Benson*

On Saturday 27th September 1958 Robert Anderson rode the 9.18am Leeds City-Middlesbrough as far as Northallerton hauled by Starbeck D49 No. 62753 *The Belvoir*.

"D49 haulage was becoming rare by then and the train went via Thirsk so this seems the likely reason for my trip. We didn't stop at Baldersby or Topcliffe and the thing I remember about the line was the ash ballast. At Northallerton, I saw 118 steam locos between 10.40am and 6.25pm and only one diesel - Type 4 No. D207. I also saw 9F 2-10-0 No. 92189 which was only 6 months old. I was surprised by the lack of A4s - only two, while A3s were the most common - 14 in all, along with seven A1s, four A2s and ten V2s." He repeated the trip on 11th October and 20th December behind 62763 with similar results although there were more trains on the latter day and no less than 21 V2s, possibly due to Christmas.

Above: Northallerton station goods yard stayed in business handling wagonload traffic until the early 1980s. In this April 1977 scene, the Class 37 has just shunted the yard and is preparing for its return to Tees marshalling yard. Besides an empty coal hopper, its train includes a 16-ton mineral wagon loaded with scrap metal. Three sidings and the cattle/goods dock remain in 2010 but for engineers' use. *Malcolm Roughley/Stephen Chapman archive*

Below: Looking south with D20 4-4-0 No. 62360 facing north in the Up Main platform while working the Northallerton Dales railtour on 4th September 1955. *Ken Hoole/Neville Stead collection.* The 1957 timetable showed Northallerton station as having a buffet which could serve "luncheons" while a second class return ticket to London cost £3 8s 8d. In 2010 the platform buildings consist only of simple brick and glass shelters while the main buildings were replaced by a single story ticket office in 1986.

Above: Northallerton station from the south with Starbeck's D49 4-4-0 No. 62765 *The Goathland* waiting in the Up bay to leave on a stopping train to Leeds. In 2010 only the two main line platforms remain while the canopies are long gone. *Neville Stead collection*

Below: Good-bye to Northallerton. A3 No. 60083 *Sir Hugo*, still sporting a single chimney, strides out of the station with an Up morning express, possibly the Sunderland to King's Cross, on 27th March 1954. The 1930s colour light signals are well in evidence. *Neville Stead collection*

Above: The spectacle of double-headed A3s about to pass Otterington with the 9.20am Delaval Sidings(Newcastle)-Holloway empty stock and parcels train on 27th March 1953. The pair are 60086 *Gainsborough*(leading) and 60075 *St. Frusquin*. Having worked the 3-coach 7.24am Leeds-West Hartlepool stopping passenger, 60086 is returning as booked from Stockton to Thirsk from where it will take a local passenger train back to Leeds. Normally a B1 4-6-0, the 7.24 from Leeds was worked by a Pacific on eight occasions in four weeks during early spring 1953. *J.W. Hague/Neville Stead collection*

In summer 1955 trains departed Otterington at 7.10am(6.27 Darlington-Doncaster - to drop off newspapers only,) 8.8am(8am Thirsk-Northallerton,) 10.11am(10.5 Northallerton-Leeds,) 12.45pm(12.39 Northallerton-Leeds,) 3.6pm(1.38 Leeds-Northallerton,) 5.14pm(5.8 Northallerton-Leeds,) and 9.17pm(8.31 Harrogate-Darlington.) There was no Sunday service. Otterington closed to passengers on 15th September 1958. Goods facilities, listed in 1956 as equipped for general goods, livestock, horse boxes and prize cattle vans but with no permanent crane, were withdrawn on 10th August 1964. Situated about a mile south of Otterington was Manor House Siding.

Below: A view which shows the fine station buildings at Otterington, rebuilt in 1932/33 to make room for the new Up Slow line, which have thankfully survived more than 50 years after closure. On 2nd September 1983 Brush Type 2 No. 31264 heads along the Up Slow with a freight consisting mainly of withdrawn Mk1 sleeping cars presumably on their way for scrap. Badly damaged by fire in 1993, the buildings and signal box have been pleasingly restored and a maroon-liveried mark 2 coach is undergoing renovation on an isolated piece of track in the former goods yard. *Peter Rose*

Above: V2 2-6-2 No. 60812 of Heaton shed speeds the Newcastle-Colchester express through Thirsk shortly after 2pm on 21st May 1959. The marshalling yards can just be made out in the left distance, beyond the gathering of spotters. Nowadays only the Slow lines have platforms, those pictured having long since been closed and graded back to give a clear path for high speed trains. The station was totally rebuilt after the Up side buildings on the right were devastated by fire in December 1987. *P.B. Booth/Neville Stead collection*

THIRSK YARD ARRIVALS & DEPARTURES
Working timetable 2nd November 1959 to 12th June 1960
am

6.47-7.5 MX	5.50 York Yard-West Hartlepool class F
10.5	7.50 class H from Malton
Untimed	10.5 class H from Low Gates
10.30	Class H to York Yard North
11.12	Light engine from Skelton New Sidings(York)
11.45	Class H to Newport Yard

pm

Untimed	Class H to Castle Hills
	Return of 10.5am from Low Gates
Untimed	Class H to Malton
	Return of 7.50am from Malton
6.20-6.40	5.51 Low Gates-York Up Yard class H
7.2-7.22	6.5 Middlesbrough Goods-Dringhouses class C
8.50-9.10	7.50 York Yard North-Low Gates class H

The 1951 Darlington District local freight working book shows a Northallerton Low Yard-Thirsk class H running in the evening and booked to leave Thirsk for Croft Yard at 10pm. It shunted Northallerton goods yard and conveyed wagons from there to Thirsk in the following order: 1) Yorks 2) Thirsk Towns 3) Normantons 4) Norths with the instruction "North traffic transferred to Down side at Thirsk and conveyed to Darlington with North traffic from Thirsk."

THIRSK YARD: Guards of trains attaching or detaching in Thirsk Yard should, before departure, advise the signalman the number of wagons and the siding into which the wagons have been attached or detached. *BR Sectional Appendix 1969*

ADVERTISED THIRSK DEPARTURES
Mondays-Fridays 17th June to 15th September 1957
am

1.13	MO	8.20pm King's Cross-Edinburgh *Set down only*
2.53	MO	7.55pm Bristol-Darlington(Catterick?) *Set down*
4.27		3.50 York-Stockton
7.21		6.27 Darlington-Doncaster
7.35		6.40 York-Edinburgh
8.36	MO	8.5 Darlington-King's Cross *15th July-26th Aug.*
8.53		6.56 Newcastle-York
9.10		6.42 Bradford Forster Square-Newcastle
10.30		9.17 Leeds-Middlesbrough
10.41		10.10 York-Edinburgh

pm

12.44	11.30 Leeds-Newcastle via Stockton
12.50	11.5 Newcastle-Leeds
1.1	12.45 Northallerton-Harrogate
2.42	10.30 Liverpool Exchange-Newcastle via Stockton
2.58	1.33 Leeds-Northallerton
4.15	2.35 Newcastle-Leeds
5.23	5.8 Northallerton-Leeds
5.37	5.10 York-Darlington
6.31	3.7 Leeds-Newcastle via Stockton
6.34	5.10 Newcastle-Liverpool Exchange
7.8	5.37 Leeds-Northallerton
7.45	5.33 Newcastle-York
8.34	6.52 FO Newcastle-Birmingham *19th July-16th Aug.*
8.40	5.0 Liverpool Lime Street-Newcastle
9.6	7.25 Newcastle-King's Cross
10.13	9.41 York-West Hartlepool

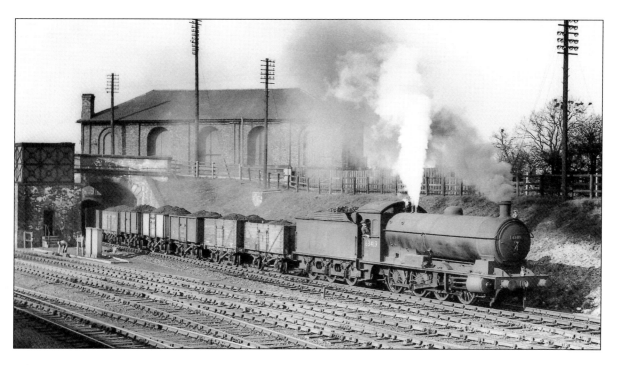

Above: With Thirsk goods shed looming above, West Hartlepool-based Q6 0-8-0 No. 63419 heads a York-bound coal train away from the station in the 1950s. The 1956 Handbook of Stations - which listed Thirsk as Thirsk Junction - stated that the goods facilities were equipped to handle all kinds of traffic except that there was no permanent crane. Goods facilities were withdrawn on 3rd October 1966. A private siding served a company listed as "Jackson's." *J.W. Hague/Neville Stead collection*

Above: English Electric Type 4 No. D254 powers away from Thirsk with the Uddingston-Cliffe empty cement tanks on 12th March 1965. *Rev. David Benson*
The northbound, and therefore loaded, working was involved in a horrific collision south of Thirsk on 31st July 1967.

In the afternoon of 31st July 1967 the Cliffe-Uddingston cement train was derailed while travelling on the Down Slow south of Thirsk. Almost immediately the 12.00 King's Cross-Aberdeen hauled by English Electric Class 50 prototype DP2 ran into the loaded wagons which were fouling the Down Fast. The sides were ripped out of some coaches; seven people died and 45 were injured. DP2 was so badly damaged it had to be written off.

The following 10.27 Bristol-Newcastle had to run round at Pilmoor and return to York. The 14.00 and 16.00 King's Cross-Edinburgh were diverted via the Settle & Carlisle and Waverley routes. But by 18.45 the closed Ripon-Northallerton line was reopened as a diversionary route for Down trains with a 30mph speed restriction north of Melmerby. With block instruments and telephones unuseable, a time interval and caution ticket system of control was used. The first train to use the diversion was that day's 18.55 King's Cross-Aberdeen Freightliner and the last was the 18.18 Kettering-Tees Yard freight on 2nd August. Up trains were able to use their normal route via the Slow line.

Left: Just south of Thirsk station, English Electric Type 4 No. D281 passes under the Thirsk Town goods branch with a Glasgow to King's Cross express on 20th May 1962. Worthy of note is the gate across the goods branch right of the bridge. *Rev. David Benson*

Above: Northallerton's veteran J25 0-6-0 No. 65720, of the original Wilson Worsdell 1898 design, at Thirsk Junction with a train returning from Thirsk Town. In the foreground is the line to Melmerby, behind the train is the ECML and beyond it the two-road engine shed. *J.W. Hague/Neville Stead collection*

Thirsk shed provided engines for shunting and local goods work in the yards and on surrounding lines. Its allocation in 1920 consisted of eleven engines: Class 398 0-6-0: 309/374; Class 59 0-6-0: 508; Class P3 0-6-0(LNER J27): 1025; Class Y 4-6-2T(LNER A7): 1170; Class 290 0-6-0T(LNER J77): 1460/1462; Class P1 0-6-0(LNER J25): 1723/1743/1973/2142. The depot closed on 1st November 1930 but was retained for watering, turning and layover of locomotives visiting with local goods and passenger workings. The shed itself stood until 1965 and the site of the depot and junction is still discernible as a patch of scrubland in 2010.

On 6th June 1973 the prototype HST reached 131mph between Northallerton and Thirsk - a new British speed record. On 11th June it reached 141mph between Thirsk and Tollerton and on 12th June it set a new world speed record for diesel traction when it reached 143mph between Otterington and Northallerton.

SHORT MEMORIES

24.4.54: D20 4-4-0 No. 62347 & J21 0-6-0 No. 65038 work the last Northallerton-Garsdale through passenger services.

25.4.54: G5 0-4-4T No. 67345 works the last passenger service from Leyburn to Northallerton.

11.8.54: G5 No. 67342 is on the 4.5pm Northallerton-Leyburn parcels.

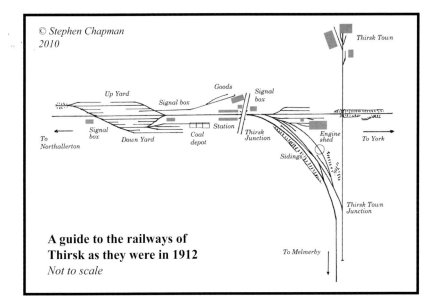

© Stephen Chapman
2010

A guide to the railways of Thirsk as they were in 1912
Not to scale

Below: Twice a day the small railway community of Pilmoor was - and still is - momentarily graced by what is probably the world's most famous train as it passed the remote station in a flash. Today, the Flying Scotsman passes Pilmoor at 125mph but even in steam days A4 No. 60017 *Silver Fox* would have been doing around 80mph with the the legendary 10 o'clock King's Cross to Edinburgh.
J.W. Hague/Neville Stead collection
On the extreme right, goods vans occupy the station's former Boroughbridge platform. The station buildings look almost Victorian in silhouette but in fact they are of the tall hipped-roof style adopted when the Down side of the station was rebuilt in the 1940s to accommodate the new Slow line to the right of 60017. When the Boroughbridge line passenger service was withdrawn in 1950, the line was severed between Pilmoor and Brafferton and the Pilmoor end used as a siding.
With no real local community to serve, Pilmoor's goods facilities were basic, being listed in the 1956 Stations Handbook as equipped to deal with only general goods. Sidings off the Boroughbridge line served a land drain pipe works until the end of the 19th century and when the works closed they were converted to handle local goods traffic and became known as Moor Siding. Goods facilities were withdrawn on 14th September 1959.

Above: Widening to four tracks has yet to be completed between Pilmoor and Alne so D20 4-4-0 No. 62388 takes to the three-track section as it passes the old Pilmoor North signal box with a West Hartlepool-York fish train in the early 1950s. The exit from the Up Slow laid in the 1940s is immediately beyond the brake van.

Although served by next to no trains each weekday, this remote station did boast a through, albeit slow, service to Edinburgh in the 1950s. Pilmoor finally gave up the ghost by closing to passengers on 5th May 1958, allowing the Up platform to make way for the new Up Slow line. In 2010 the only sign of a station having been here is the 1940s station master's house on the Down side.

Below: Original B16 4-6-0 No. 61460 passes what was then Pilmoor South signal box with an Up Through Freight. *Both J.W. Hague/Neville Stead collection*

In summer 1950, trains departed Pilmoor at 7.34am(6.25 Darlington-Doncaster,) 7.36am (6.55 York-Darlington,) 8.6am(to Boroughbridge and Harrogate,) 12.38pm SO(11.35 Darlington-York,) 1.28pm SO, 6.16pm, 8.48pm SO(all to Boroughbridge and Harrogate.) In summer 1955, Pilmoor departures were: 7.16am(6.40 York-Edinburgh,) 7.34am(6.27 Darlington-Doncaster,) 12.52pm(unadvertised stop to take up only by the 11am Newcastle-Leeds,) and 6.18pm(5pm Leeds-Newcastle.)

Above: Passengers on passing ECML trains may have been bemused by the apparent bus shelter perched on a disused railway embankment standing at right angles to the west of the main line just south of Pilmoor. The shelter was for the benefit of locomen taking eyesight tests and the embankment was the abortive connection between the Boroughbridge and Malton lines. York D49/1 "Shire" 4-4-0 No. 62702 *Oxfordshire,* an incredibly ancient six-wheeled coach and Gresley corridor brake appear to be "wrong road" on the Down Fast at Pilmoor South but they are reversing after bringing a party of locomen for eyesight testing. *Ken Hoole/Neville Stead colln.*

SHORT MEMORIES

23-25.10.54 & 30.10-1.11.54: A minor bridge north of Ripon station with outer cast iron girders dating from 1847 is reconstructed in pre-cast concrete. York and Darlington breakdown cranes are present along with K1 2-6-0 No. 62008, J39 0-6-0 No. 64857 and O4 2-8-0 No. 63665 on the first weekend. No. 62008, another O4 & B16 4-6-0 No. 61471 are there on the second weekend.

21.11.54: A3 Pacifics Nos. 60103 *Flying Scotsman* and 60110 *Robert the Devil,* both of Leicester Central, pass through Ripon when Up ECML trains are diverted due to track relaying.

Below: Relief signalman Jeff Lumb looks on as the photographer's son David Rose studies the panel inside Pilmoor box during an official visit on 13th April 1979. This box replaced the old Sessay Wood box in 1933, was renamed Pilmoor South in 1943 and became just Pilmoor when signalling was modernized and Pilmoor North abolished after the widening in 1960. This box was closed in 1985. *Peter Rose*

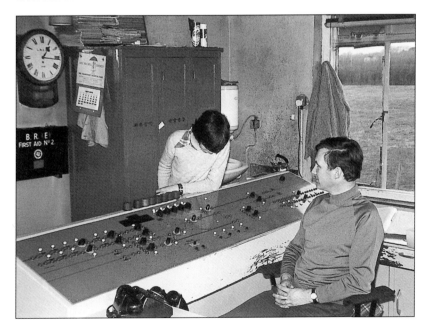

Above: At the opposite end of the scale to the Pacifics and their famous express trains, Y3 Sentinel shunter No. 68155 trundles past Bishophouse Junction as it heads for home after a visit to Darlington Works. Home being 53D Bridlington, it is apparently taking the long way round via York rather than the more direct Malton line in the background. The line curving away to the right is the Bishophouse-Sunbeck curve used by the York-Pickering service. *Neville Stead collection*

Below: Two and three quarter miles south of Pilmoor, A4 No. 60033 *Seagull* speeds effortlessly through Raskelf station with a southbound express in the early 1950s. In wartime, Raskelf served Tholthorpe airfield two miles to the west as well as Tholthorpe village another mile further on and the village of Raskelf itself which was a mile to the east. *Neville Stead collection*

In summer 1950 Raskelf was served by trains departing at: 7.25am(6.55 York-Darlington,) 7.40am (6.25 Darlington-Doncaster,) 7.48am(7.25 York-Pickering,) 8.27am(7.10 Pickering-York,) 10.58am(10.30 York-Pickering,) 11.32am(10.15 Pickering-York,) 12.44pm SO(11.35 Darlington-York,) and 6.28pm(6pm York-Pickering.) By summer 1955 only two called there - the 6.40am York-Edinburgh at 7.10 and the 6.27am Darlington-Doncaster at 7.40, their main purpose probably to deliver newspapers and mail. No trains called there on Sundays. Closure to passengers came on 6th May 1958. The goods depot, which in 1956 was listed as equipped to handle only general goods, livestock, horse boxes and prize cattle vans with no permanent crane, stayed in business until August 1964. Hodgson's coal merchants had their own siding.

Above: The next station going towards York, just two miles south of Raskelf, was Alne, the junction with the Easingwold Railway. V2 2-6-2 No. 60854 hides the Easingwold bay platform as it races through with an Up express in the mid-1950s. Alne village was about a mile to the west. *J.W. Hague/Neville Stead collection*

Below: School cap, blazer and short trousers were standard gear for boys in the 1950s, whether in school or not - well, there wasn't much else to choose from! This youngster is easily compensated though for the lack of trendy designer clothes by the sight of A1 No. 60154 *Bon Accord* as it glides a southbound express swiftly through Alne station on its roller bearing driving axles in the late 1950s. The Up side platform, its modernistic buildings, the footbridge and Easingwold bay would all be swept away within a couple of years to make room for the new Up Slow line. In 2010 it is almost impossible to spot the sites of some of these smaller stations - especially when passing at 125mph. *J.W. Hague/Neville Stead collection*

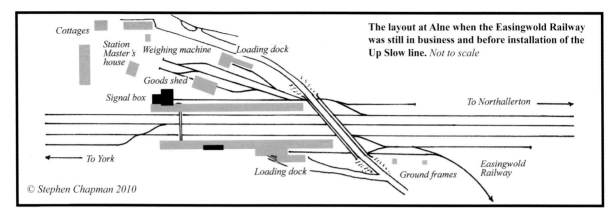

The layout at Alne when the Easingwold Railway was still in business and before installation of the Up Slow line. *Not to scale*

Cottages

Station Master's house

Weighing machine

Loading dock

Goods shed

Signal box

To Northallerton

To York

Loading dock

Ground frames

Easingwold Railway

© Stephen Chapman 2010

One of the better-served small stations, trains departed Alne on weekdays in summer 1950 at: 7.20am(6.55 York-Darlington,) 7.45am(6.25 Darlington-Doncaster,) 8.32am(7.10 Pickering-York,) 8.49am(8.30 York-Newcastle,) 10.53am(10.30 York-Pickering,) 11.37am(10.15 Pickering-York,) 12.53pm SO(11.35am Darlington-York,) 6.23pm (6pm York-Pickering,) 7.6pm(5.40 Pickering-York,) 7.12pm(6.45 York-Newcastle,) 8.6pm(5.30 Newcastle-York.) On Sundays, trains called at 7.12am (6.45 York-Newcastle,) 9.14am(6.54 Newcastle-Doncaster,) 8.20pm(6pm Newcastle-York.) Alne closed to passengers on 5th May 1958. Goods facilities were also superior to other small stations, being listed in 1956 as able to handle all classes of traffic and equipped with a one-ton crane. They were withdrawn on 10th August 1964.

Above: One other railway in the locality, which worked into the late 1980s, was a 2ft gauge line at the Alne Brick Co. for carrying clay from the claypit to the works. This view shows the claycutter and the narrow gauge track early in 1976. *Stephen Chapman*

Below: The end of the line for Easingwold's very own railway, affectionately known as "T'Awd Coffeepot." At the end of the 2.5-mile light railway from Alne, J72 0-6-0T No. 68698 stands in the station with a BR brake and parcels van on the last day of services, 27th December 1957. *Neville Stead collection.*

Right: Until 1947, the Easingwold Railway had its own locomotive. Maroon-liveried Hudswell, Clarke 0-6-0ST No. 2 built in 1903, works No. 608, and rebuilt in 1924 was the railway's third loco. She is seen at Darlington Works most likely in 1947, the occasion when it was found the new boiler and firebox she needed would cost too much. She was replaced by a loco hired from BR at York and scrapped in 1948/9.

Normally pottering back and forth with the railway's single ex-North Eastern Railway 6-wheeled coach (minus its centre wheels) she was, on one occasion, required to perform above and beyond the call of duty. That was when a children's excursion ran throughout from Easingwold to Liverpool and No. 2 had to reach the main line with five LNER bogie coaches in tow. *Neville Stead colln.*

Below: A view of Easingwold station and its timber buildings on 23rd June 1957. There is something missing from the quality of 21st century life when such pockets of charm and character capable of performing a useful service have been swept aside in the name of profit and cold, featureless efficiency. The Easingwold Railway closed to passengers on 29th November 1948 and to parcels and goods with effect from 30th December 1957. The station survived until destroyed by fire in 1967. A small housing estate now occupies this spot. *Neville Stead collection*

The 1956 Handbook of Stations showed Easingwold as able to handle all classes of freight, including parcels but there was no permanent crane. As well as agricultural traffic, sugar beet and incoming coal, its chief revenue came from transporting day-old chicks to Alne where they were transferred to main line trains for delivery across the country. A little-used siding was located at Crankley Lane level crossing, about half-way along the line. Normally, two goods trains ran each weekday on Mondays to Fridays with one on Saturdays.

Above: Resting at the Easingwold buffer stop on 23rd June 1957 is a special train run for the Railway Correspondence and Travel Society using BR open wagons and J71 0-6-0T No. 68246, one of the locos hired from BR to work everyday traffic. The Railway Hotel on the left remains in 2010 as a reminder of this remarkable little railway but as a private dwelling.

Neville Stead collection

The September 1945 Meccano Magazine gave an account by Mr. E.W. Petchey of a journey along the Easingwold Railway. He reported: "The train was headed by the line's only engine, No. 2, a saddle tank built by Hudswell, Clarke & Co. Ltd., in 1903. Behind this were a main line cattle wagon and the Easingwold company's ex-NER ancient four-wheeled coach, boasting one first class and two second class compartments, as well as a section for guard and packages. There is no continuous braking system; the track is formed mostly of flat-bottomed rails and appeared to be considerably overgrown with grass and weeds. The other passengers were regular travellers for whom the driver waited if necessary, blowing his whistle meanwhile! The maximum number of advertised journeys per day at present is three each way; seven or more were operated in 1939, so the service may soon improve."

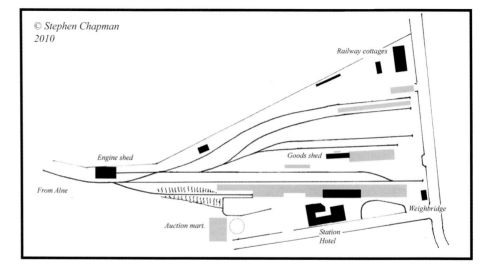

© Stephen Chapman 2010

Railway cottages

Engine shed

Goods shed

From Alne

Weighbridge

Auction mart.

Station Hotel

Right: The layout of Easingwold station.

Not to scale

Above: A mere one a half miles south of Alne and nine and three quarter miles from York, came Tollerton station where A3 No. 60060 *The Tetrarch* is passing the derelict station buildings with an Up class C fully-fitted express freight in 1963. Despite appearances, the station was still open to passengers and remained so until 1st November 1965. The section from Alne was widened in NER days, hence the older buildings. *Jack Wild/Stephen Chapman archive*

Below: A2/2 Pacific No. 60501 *Cock o' the North* - a 1943 Thompson rebuild of Gresley's Class P2 2-8-2 - slams through Tollerton station with a 1950s northbound express from the London Midland Region. The station buildings and the original signal box are on the right. *Neville Stead collection*

In summer 1950 Tollerton was served by trains which departed at: 7.15am(6.55 York-Darlington,) 7.41am(7.25 York-Pickering,) 7.49am(6.25 Darlington-Doncaster,) 10.48am(10.30 York-Pickering,) 11.42am(10.15 Pickering-York,) 12.53pm SO(11.35 Newcastle-York,) 6.18pm(6pm York-Pickering,) 7.12pm(5.40 Pickering-York.) There was no Sunday service. By summer 1955, with the Pickering trains gone, just two trains called there, the 6.40am York-Edinburgh at 7am and the 6.27am Darlington-Doncaster at 7.49, presumably for delivering newspapers and mail - they certainly wouldn't be much use to passengers. By summer 1960, the 6.40am York-Edinburgh was Tollerton's only train. For years the service hadn't even offered a day trip to York and back. It's amazing how the station managed to stay open another five years.

Above: Displaying class 7 disc headcode, Brush Type 2 No. 5543 passes the remains of Tollerton station on the Up Slow with a long train of empty mineral wagons on 24th June 1972. The siding on the right leads into the goods yard which had been retained for use by the engineers' department. Although goods facilities were rather basic with no permanent crane, Tollerton was listed in 1956 as able to handle all classes of freight. They were withdrawn on 6th September 1965 but one siding, containing an old engineers brake van, survived in 2010, a second siding serving the loading dock was also still in situ but disconnected. *Peter Rose*

Below: Tollerton power box, being passed by a Class 47-hauled northbound special on the same day as above, was commissioned in January 1961. It controlled 12 route miles and new signalling included automatic signals which could be manually controlled by the Tollerton signalman when required. Together with the modernized box at Pilmoor(formerly Pilmoor South) it enabled closure of the boxes at Raskelf, Alne, Sunbeck, Pilmoor North and Sessay. *Peter Rose*

It was in the shallow cutting just south of Tollerton, in a section controlled by semi-automatic colour light signals, that over a hundred passengers and the crew of A1 Pacific No. 60153 had a lucky escape on 5th June 1950.

It was the hottest day of the summer so far and the temperature in the shade reached 82 degrees fahrenheit. The rail temperature soared to 112 degrees. No. 60153, only built in August 1949 and having run just 66,000 miles, was heading the 12.15pm Newcastle-York express along the Up Main when it hit a section of rail which had buckled in the heat. It was only doing around 45mph due to signal checks but 60153 was derailed, thrown across the Up Slow and finished up leaning over at an angle of 45 degrees. One side was torn off the first coach - a corridor brake third - and its wooden body detached from its welded steel frame. Along with the second coach which was also extensively damaged, it was strewn across the Down Main and Slow lines. The third coach was also badly damaged, while the fourth, a restaurant car, was also derailed. All these vehicles were wooden bodied. Driver W. A. Streeton, fireman B. Carr and nine passengers were taken to hospital but later released.

Only moments before, the Up Flying Scotsman with driver W. Errington, fireman T. Atkinson and guard G.S.F. Olney in charge had passed over the same stretch of rail at 65mph without being derailed. It had to stop near Beningbrough, however, because the last two coaches had been damaged, one of them, it later transpired, with distortion to the bogie solebars.

Passenger trains were diverted via Ripon and freight held back until all lines were cleared only 22 hours later.

Presiding over the Ministry of Transport inquiry into the accident, railway inspecting officer Col. D. McMullen reported that the main cause of the derailment was track buckling due to the fishplates at the rail joints not having been slackened in readiness for hot weather.

"The derailment of the 12.15pm express was, clearly, brought about by the buckling of the track as the rear coaches of the preceeding train, the Flying Scotsman, passed over it. The rails were unable to expand on a very hot day and were therefore subject to undue compression."

It only needed, he continued, the thrust and vibration of a fast train to release the locked up stress, allowing the track to overcome the resistance of the ballast which at that point was insufficient to hold the track in place under such circumstances.

"It was the "freezing" of the fishplates to the rails which prevented expansion, in spite of the fishplates having been oiled, because the fishbolts had not been slackened."

He also remarked that the accident might have been averted if Tollerton signal box had not been switched out. "On long stretches of line with signals working automatically, an emergency may require a train to be stopped between permanently open signal boxes, as in this case. Some means which would enable the signalman to put all signals to danger in rear of his box does, therefore, appear desirable."

Col. Mc. Mullen congratulated Driver Streeton and fireman Carr for their prompt action, despite their injuries, in protecting the lines.

Passing the nine milepost and in the shallow cutting close to where the 12.15pm Newcastle-York came to grief, freshly outshopped Leeds Neville Hill D49/2 4-4-0 No. 62756 *The Brocklesby* **heads a Down stopping passenger train in the late 1940s.**
The late Ernest Sanderson/Stephen Chapman archive

Above: At Warehill bridge - the same spot and on the same occasion as the previous picture, B1 4-6-0 No. 61022 *Sassaby* is allowed to trundle its loose-coupled Through Freight along the Down Main. In 1964 the telegraph poles lining the route became just a back-up for one of the most advanced microwave telecommunications systems anywhere. *The late Ernest Sanderson/Stephen Chapman archive*

Below: The platforms have been mostly removed and the 1930s Down side shelter stands alone in this view looking north at Beningbrough station, four and a quarter miles south of Tollerton and five and a half miles north of York. It is 19th March 1963 and a somewhat grubby looking V2 2-6-2 No. 60812 passes the goods sidings as it heads for York with an Up class H coke train. *Peter Rose*

Above: Beningbrough station(Shipton until 1898) in the late 1940s with Heaton-based A3 No. 60073 *St. Gatien* **heading a northbound express. The goods yard is just visible behind the Up platform on the left while the 1930s signal box protrudes above the locomotive's tender.** *The late Ernest Sanderson/Stephen Chapman archive*

In summer 1950, Beningbrough was served by the following departures: 7.5am(6.55 York-Darlington,) 7.57am(6.25 Darlington-Doncaster,) 10.40am(10.30 York-Pickering,) 11.50am(10.15 Pickering-York,) 1.1pmSO(11.35am Darlington-York,) 6.10pm(6pm York-Pickering,) 7.20pm(5.40 Pickering-York.) There was no Sunday service. The station closed to passengers on 15th September 1958. Goods facilities were listed in the 1956 Stations Handbook as being able to handle all classes of freight but with no permanent crane. Downgraded to a public delivery siding(an unstaffed depot where customers mainly loaded and unloaded their own traffic in wagonloads only) when the station closed to passengers, the goods yard closed altogether on 5th July 1965.

Right: The station buildings and remains of the Up platform at Beningbrough are evident in this shot of V2 No. 60972 heading north on 19th March 1963 with a parcels and mixed stock train, the first vehicle of which is a horse box. The remaining portion of platform was still there in 2010. *Peter Rose*

Above: Just south of Beningbrough and 200 miles from Edinburgh where it began its journey, Deltic No. 55013 *The Black Watch* speeds the 09.50 Edinburgh-Plymouth towards York on 27th June 1981. There the Deltic working this service handed it over to a Class 47, or sometimes a Class 50 returning to the Western Region after overhaul at Doncaster Works. *Stephen Chapman*

Below: Examples of the automatic searchlight signals installed on this stretch of the main line by the LNER. A K3 2-6-0 passes Down 3B(Main and Slow) signals while working an Up class E express freight in the 1940s. *The late Ernest Sanderson/Stephen Chapman archive.*

Above: On the outskirts of York and with the village of Skelton across the fields on the left, A3 No. 60040 *Cameronian* gets into its stride with a northbound express composed mainly of London Midland stock in early BR days. The first coach has to be of interest to coaching stock experts. *The late Ernest Sanderson/Stephen Chapman archive*

Below: The same location as above but from the opposite side and more than 30 years later. English Electric Type 4(Class 40) No. 40113 heads a northbound train of tanks along the Down Slow on 18th August 1981. Within 10 years this scene would have changed even more dramatically - the Class 40s were no more and the line had been electrified. *Stephen Chapman*

Above: Pure Leeds Northern and a reminder of the kind of traffic this now abandoned line once carried. In the mid-1950s Starbeck **D49/2 4-4-0 No. 62753** *The Belvoir* **pilots A3 No. 60074** *Harvester* **and its heavy 12-coach Newcastle-Liverpool express up the bank at Monkton Moor, about three miles south of Ripon.** *Both pictures on this page J.W. Hague/Neville Stead collection*

Below: The two boys beside the River Ure seem oblivious to the rumbling overhead as well polished **B16/1 4-6-0 No. 61478** and **D49/1 4-4-0 No. 62730** *Berkshire* **stride onto Ripon Viaduct while leaving the station with what could be the same train as above.**

Above: The Queen of Scots Pullman was without doubt the most important train to run over the Leeds-Northallerton section of the Leeds Northern. The northbound train is about to pass Ripon station as it rolls off the River Ure viaduct with Deltic No. D9000 *Royal Scots Grey* at the head on 20th March 1963. *Rev. David Benson*

Below: A pair of J39 0-6-0s, Starbeck's No. 64821 leading, find themselves elevated to the glorious task of powering the southbound Queen of Scots through Ripon on 10th May 1956 after the train's A2 Pacific had failed. *J.W. Hague/Neville Stead collection.*
Ripon station was a good three quarters of a mile north of the city centre and was actually situated in a locality known as Ure Bank, north of the river. Its facilities included a buffet which the summer 1950 timetable advertised as serving "breakfasts, luncheons and teas." By summer 1957 it had become one of a dozen similarly-sized North Eastern Region stations to have a privately-run buffet.

RIPON PASSENGER TRAINS
Weekdays 13th June-18th September 1955

am

1.30 MO	1.15 from Thirsk *Unadvertised*
1.35 MO	Empty stock to Harrogate
2.53	2am Leeds City-Newcastle news
5.3	3.52 from Leeds City
5.8	Empty stock to Northallerton
7.3-6	5.56 Leeds-Thirsk
7.35-39	7.10 Northallerton-Leeds City
8.26-30	8.2 Thirsk-Leeds City
8.36-9	7.24 Leeds-West Hartlepool
9.20	Empty stock from Harrogate
9.56 SO	6.10 Nottingham Midland-Craigendoran
	Until 3rd Sept. Unadvertised
10.5 SO	9.6 Leeds-Newcastle
10.11-14	9.17 Leeds City-Middlesbrough
10.18	10.18 Ripon-King's Cross
10.24-27	8.55 Newcastle-Liverpool
10.25-27	9.35 Leeds City-Saltburn
	Saturdays Only. 2nd July-27th August
10.44-46	10.5 Northallerton-Leeds City
11.24-26 SO	10.16 West Hartlepool-Blackpool
	16th July-20th August
11.33-36 MFO	10.2 Sunderland-Manchester Exchange
11.33-36 SO	9.35 South Shields-Manchester Exchange
11.45 MFSO	9.30 Manchester Exchange-Newcastle

pm

12.2-12.5	9am Liverpool Lime St.-Newcastle
12.7 SO	10.40 Saltburn-Manchester Exchange
	Until 27th August
1.4 SO	11.30 Newcastle-Llandudno
	2nd July to 27th August
1.19-23	12.39 Northallerton-Leeds City

2.20-23 SO	9.15am Llandudno-Newcastle
	Until 3rd September
2.34-37	1.38 Leeds City-Northallerton
2.44-47	2.5 Darlington-Leeds City
3.32	10.50 Glasgow-King's Cross
	The Queen of Scots
3.38 MSX	10.18 from King's Cross
3.55 MSX	Empty stock to Harrogate
4.0 MSO	10.35 from King's Cross
4.15	12.5 King's Cross-Glasgow
	The Queen of Scots
4.18 MSO	Empty stock to Harrogate
4.41 SO	1.5 Blackpool Central-West Hartlepool
	23rd July-27th August
5.1-3	3.50 Leeds-Northallerton
5.10-12 SO	2.6 Liverpoo Lime St.-Newcastle
5.23-25	2.20 Liverpool Lime St.-Newcastle
5.44-46 FO	4.10 Sunderland-Liverpool Exchange
5.50-53	5.8 Northallerton-Leeds City
6.0 FSX	5.35 light engine from Starbeck shed
6.12-15	4.15 Newcastle-Liverpool Lime St.
6.27 SO	12.12 Craigendoran-Nottingham Midland
	Until 10th September. Unadvertised
6.32-5	6.15 Harrogate-Thirsk *6.39-42 on Sats*
7.56-8 FSO	5.38 Manchester Exchange-Newcastle
8.6-8	7.42 Thirsk-Harrogate
8.46-8	8.31 Harrogate-Darlington
9.5-10	8.40 Northallerton-Leeds
9.55	9.38 from Harrogate
10.6	Empty stock to Harrogate
11.7-14 SO	10pm Leeds City-Thirsk

Passing times of non-stop trains shown in italics

Below: The layout at Ripon as it was in the early 20th century. *Not to scale*

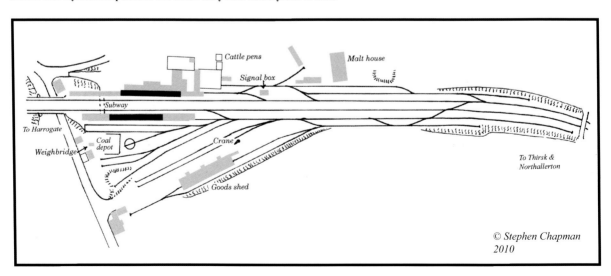

© Stephen Chapman
2010

Below: With Ripon goods sidings on the left, an unidentified and as yet un-named Deltic, possibly D9010 or D9019, heads the north-bound Queen of Scots through the station in January 1963. The 3,300hp Deltic is dwarfed by the large station house beyond which are the single-storey station buildings that were fronted by a tall Gothic-style three-arched entrance said to have been designed to reflect the city's cathedral. The buildings survive in 2010 as private dwellings. *Jack Wild/Stephen Chapman archive*

Above: K1 2-6-0 No. 62026, allocated to 52C Blaydon shed on Tyneside, pulls out of Ripon with what is probably a Leeds-Newcastle express in the late 1950s. The goods shed and yard crane can just be seen on the left. *J.W. Hague/Neville Stead collection*

Below: Sentinel steam railcar No. 2268 *Emerald* at the north end of Ripon station some time in the 1930s. The Sentinel railcars were the LNER's attempt to cut costs on branch lines at a time when they were losing passengers to buses but on this occasion *Emerald* had been providing a connection to Ripon for passengers off the northbound Queen of Scots. A Great Western Railway wagon stands in the siding on the right. *J.W. Hague/Neville Stead collection*

Above: Railcars of a more recent kind. A Metro-Cammell DMU passes Ripon signal box and the Down sidings as it approaches the station with a Leeds-bound service in March 1964. *Jack Wild/Stephen Chapman archive*

Below: An Up express service in the charge of B1 4-6-0 No. 61353 approaches Ripon station in the late 1950s.
J.W. Hague/Neville Stead collection

Above: Empty coaching stock, possibly for a races special returning to Leeds, approaches Ripon station headed by Starbeck D49/2 4-4-0 No. 62755 *The Bilsdale* **piloting J39 0-6-0 No. 64922.** *J.W. Hague/Neville Stead collection*

Below: J25 0-6-0 No. 65726 displays class H headlamps as it sits in the Up sidings behind the station on 12th September 1959, having arrived with the last pick-up to be worked by Starbeck shed. *Neville Stead*

Above: York B1 No. 61021 *Reitbok*, **shorn of its nameplates and with the name painted on, shunts the pick-up on 4th January 1966. The pick-up was worked by York after the closure of Starbeck shed in September 1959.** *Rev. David Benson*

The 1956 Handbook of Stations listed Ripon as equipped to handle all classes of freight with a maximum permanent cranage capacity of 5 tons. A private siding was the A.G.B. Allton & Co. Ltd. Ebor Concrete Siding while there were also sidings at Littlethorpe, about two miles south of Ripon. Ripon closed to goods traffic with effect from 5th September 1969.

Right: Railwaymen with 350hp 0-6-0 diesel shunter (Class 08) No. D3313 during a visit of the pick-up to Ripon.

From left are two shunters, the driver and his mate - all from York - three Ripon goods depot staff and on the right, David Benson working as a labourer during his student days.

The Reverend David Benson had first hand knowledge of the railway at Ripon. His father was goods inspector there and he himself worked at the goods depot for a time. He recalls the kind of traffic handled by Ripon and doubtless many similar depots across North and East Yorkshire.

"During my national service with the RAF from 1954 to 1956 my dad, Len Benson, was promoted from goods foreman at Tadcaster to goods inspector at Ripon, my parents moving from Boston Spa - my birthplace - to Sharow village, just a short bike ride to Ripon goods yard.

"Prior to my starting my theological studies at Durham University, I was 'employed' by my dad at the goods yard in summer 1957. It was a very busy enterprise, and I suspect quite profitable for BR. There was a warehouse for mixed goods, a cattle dock and a four or five bay coal stage whose profits perhaps enhanced the station master's salary - his name was Mr. King. Opposite the coal staging were two very large stores containing all manner of feed stuff for farm animals. I became quite skilled at knowing the difference between calf and sow weaner pellets! There was a steady procession of tractors and trailers which pulled alongside the stores. Some of the regulars would repair to my dad's office for a cuppa whilst yours truly loaded their trailers - I never heard of any sows dying from being fed the wrong food!

"The highlight of each day was the arrival of the pick-up goods- I don't know whether it originated from Starbeck or York. On one occasion it was pulled by B1 No. 61021 *Reitbok*, minus its nameplates. At other times, Class 08 diesel shunter No. D3313 did the honours.

"In the warehouse, taking good care of the items in the vans were four stout fellows with years of experience under their belts. Principal checker was Fred who, in broadest Yorkshire called out, and duly recorded each item. The one I remember went like this: "Woolworths - fower" - four parcels for Woolworths in the city. Taking part in this colourful crew were Tommy Guite, John Trattles and a gentleman by the name of Walt - all gently supervised by my father. As I recall, the said items were collected from the staging and delivered by road into the city and surrounding countryside by one of those wonderful three-wheeled Scammell "horses."

"Quite a lot of goods for the Masham area were conveyed by the pick-up after visiting Ripon. It used to trundle up via Tanfield to the end of the branch line where there was also an army camp.

"Ripon was on the main artery from the ECML at Northallerton which could allow through trains to Harrogate, York, Leeds and Doncaster. This diversionary route was particularly valuable when freight trains regularly scattered their wagons all across the ECML between York and Northallerton. It was such a valuable section of track that Dr. Beeching closed it!

"On my dad's days off from goods yard duty I was able to spend some time on the station. There was always a steady procession of freight trains - largely conveying steel from the Teeside works. Important through trains between Newcastle and Liverpool generally had a Neville Hill A3 on the Leeds-Newcastle leg, 60036 *Colombo* being a regular. The Queen of Scots graced Ripon in both directions on its drawn out journey between London and Glasgow. Again an A3 was usually allocated, until the Deltics took over.

"Northallerton can be a draughty station and none more so when it rains. My April 19th 1963 visit was such a day. Most of the principal passenger trains were diesel-hauled, except for A1 No. 60151 *Midlothian* on a King's Cross-Newcastle and A4 No. 60020 *Guillemot* on a Cardiff-Newcastle. The Flying Scotsman and Queen of Scots were both Deltic-hauled by D9018 *Ballymoss* and D9009 *Alycidon* respectively. A4 No. 60005 *Sir Charles Newton*, in a bedraggled state, was relegated to freight work.

"The closure of Ripon brought my dad's redeployment. He was offered a station master's post somewhere along the line from Inverness to Kyle of Lochalsh. My mother, who sadly never liked travelling - they could have toured the land on Privilege tickets - definitely didn't fancy living in the wilds of Ross & Cromarty so after 41 years' devoted service to the railways he retired and took his gold wrist watch, which I still use, and £200."

Left: **Ripon goods warehouse staff in the late 1950s. They are, from left: Fred, the checker, Tommy Guite, John Trattles, one member of the staff whose name escapes and, on the right, inspector Len Benson.**
Rev. David Benson

Melmerby Ministry of Supply depot was connected to the Leeds Northern line by a triangle, the north curve from Melmerby North (as in the picture above right) and the south curve from Melmerby South. In September 1955, the north curve which had been out of use for some years, was removed along with all points and signals connected with it, leaving the south curve as the only connection.

Above: Melmerby, three miles north of Ripon, was the junction between the original Leeds & Thirsk Railway and the 'new' line direct to Northallerton as well as the branch to Masham. It served the village of Wath, half a mile to the west, as well as Melmerby, half a mile to the east. The southbound Queen of Scots hauled by A3 No. 60081 *Shotover* passes the three-way splitting signal protecting the Down approach to the junction, the arm on the right being for Thirsk, the middle arm for Northallerton and the left arm for Masham. *J.W. Hague/Neville Stead collection*

Below: Starbeck D49 4-4-0 No. 62745 *The Hurworth* passes Melmerby North signal box as it comes off the Thirsk line with a local train to Leeds in the mid-1950s. Melmerby was a "three-pronged" station with two platforms on the Thirsk line, two on the Northallerton line and one on the Down side for Masham. *J.W. Hague/Neville Stead collection*
The 1956 Handbook of Stations listed Melmerby as having a 5-ton permanent crane and equipped to handle all classes of freight. It closed to public goods traffic on 27th July 1964 but a private siding continued to serve the Ministry of Supply depot.

Above: In this classic North Eastern scene shortly after nationalisation, D20 4-4-0 No. 62363 enters Baldersby station with a Thirsk-Leeds class B service. As can be seen, the Up line was being used for storing surplus wagons at the time while the Down line was being worked as a single line. The storage of surplus wagons in this way was a feature of lightly-used branch lines across the county between the 1940s and 1960s. *J.W. Hague/Neville Stead collection*

Below: The Melmerby-Thirsk line was once part of the Leeds Northern main line but had been reduced to branch line status since the start of the 20th century. By the time of this picture the Up line had been blocked out of use for wagon storage. Starbeck's D49 No. 62755 *The Bilsdale* passes Baldersby station with a Down class A service, possibly the 9.17am Leeds-Middlesbrough. The distant bridge carries the A1 over the line. *J.W. Hague/Neville Stead collection*

Baldersby was listed in the 1956 Stations Handbook as able to handle all classes of traffic and equipped with a 3-ton permanent crane. It closed to all traffic along with the line which served it on 14th September 1959.

MELMERBY-THIRSK PASSENGER TRAINS SUMMER 1955

12.35am MO Topcliffe-Thirsk empty stock
1.15am MO Thirsk-Ripon class A non-stop *Unadvertised*
5.8am Ripon-Northallerton empty stock
5.56am Leeds City-Thirsk class B(calling Baldersby 7.17, Topcliffe 7.22)
8.2am Thirsk-Leeds City class B(calling Topcliffe 8.7, Baldersby 8.16)
9.17am Leeds City-Middlesbrough class A(non-stop Melmerby-Thirsk)
10.5am Northallerton-Leeds City class B(calling Topcliffe 10.21, Baldersby 10.35)
12.39pm Northallerton-Leeds City class B(calling Topcliffe 1pm, Baldersby 1.9)
1.38pm Leeds City-Northallerton class A(calling Topcliffe 2.50(2.52 SO)
5.8pm Northallerton-Leeds City class B(calling Topcliffe 5.28, Baldersby 5.38)
6.15pm Harrogate-Thirsk class B(calling Baldersby 6.46, Topcliffe 6.51)
7.42pm Thirsk-Harrogate class B(calling Topcliffe 7.47, Baldersby 7.56)
8.31pm Harrogate-Darlington class A(calling Topcliffe 9.2)
10pm SO Leeds City-Thirsk class B(calling Baldersby 11.25, Topcliffe 11.30)

Sundays

9.30am Leeds City-Thirsk class A (calling Topcliffe 10.35)
11.35am Thirsk-Leeds Central class A(calling Topcliffe 11.40)
5.20pm Leeds City-Thirsk class A(non-stop Ripon-Thirsk)
7.30pm Thirsk-Leeds City class B(calling Topcliffe 7.35 and Baldersby 7.44)
7.48pm Harrogate-Thirsk class A(calling Baldersby 8.17 and Topcliffe 8.23)
9.20pm Thirsk-Leeds City class B(calling Topcliffe 9.25)
11.15pm Leeds City-Topcliffe class A(arr 12.25am Monday)

It can be gleaned from the above how local passenger services on this and other lines were geared to the needs of the airforce and army camps that were scattered around the area at that time, especially Topcliffe in this case.

In 1956 Topclife was listed as having a 1.5-ton crane and able to handle general goods, livestock and horse boxes and prize cattle vans. It too closed completely on 14th September 1959.

Below: Untypical motive power for a Leeds Northern local service. Farnley Junction's ex-LMS Stanier Class 5 4-6-0 No. 45075 crosses the A167 at Topcliffe with a class B stopping train from Thirsk in the 1950s.
Topcliffe station was in the middle of nowhere, the village being two and a quarter miles to the south and the RAF camp a mile beyond that.
J.W. Hague/Neville Stead collection

Above: The elegance of the D20 class is shown to good effect in this view of Starbeck's No. 62389 leaving Thirsk with a local service for Ripon and Leeds in early BR days. *J.W. Hague/Neville Stead collection*

Above: Thirsk Town Junction looking towards Melmerby in March 1966. Since the early 20th century - and possibly before that - there had been no direct access to Thirsk Town from the Melmerby line. Instead, freight workings reached the junction via the line on the right which is a siding from Thirsk Junction. They then reversed to gain the left hand line to Thirsk Town. Prior to being lifted some years before, the double track running lines of the Melmerby route had occupied the overgrown space to the right of the siding. *Jack Wild/Stephen Chapman archive*

The Thirsk Town branch, stated the 1960 BR North Eastern Region Sectional Appendix, was 1 mile 1430yds long from the junction at Thirsk main line station and was worked according to One Engine in Steam regulations with a maximum line speed of 10mph in both directions.

The 1956 Handbook of Stations listed Thirsk Town as having a maximum permanent cranage capacity of 5 tons and able to handle general goods and furniture vans, carriages, motor cars, portable engines and machines on wheels.

There were no less than four private sidings. They served Esso Petroleum, Shell-Mex & BP, the Ministry of Agriculture, Fisheries & Food store, and J. Toes. Strike & Sons had a private siding between Thirsk and Topcliffe.

Above: With traffic from the Shell-Mex & BP siding evident, BR Standard Class 2 2-6-0 No. 78015 from Northallerton shed crosses the ECML with a Thirsk Town trip working in the late 1950s. *J.W. Hague/Neville Stead collection*

Right: The approach to Thirsk Town as it was on the last day before closure which took place with effect from 3rd October 1966. *Jack Wild/ Stephen Chapman archive*

THIRSK TOWN BRANCH The working of freight trains on this branch to and from Toes' standage at the dead end of the branch is as follows:-

  Inward Trains - The train must proceed cautiously toward the dead end and clear of the connection with the sidings, from which point it must be propelled to Thirsk Town Goods Station.

  Outward Trains - The train must be propelled from the Goods Station to the dead end and when the locomotive is clear of the Siding connection the train must draw forward to No.32 Subsidiary Signal and thence to the Down Marshalling Yard.

  Toes' Standage - not more than two wagons for Mr. Toes may be propelled in front of the locomotive from the Down Marshalling Yard to the Standage Point allocated to Mr. Toes at the dead end of the Thirsk Town branch.

  Wagons from the Standage must be attached to the Guard's van on the Down journey and drawn outside the van to the Down Marshalling Yard.

  No shunting must be done at the Standage.

  If when wagons are propelled from Thirsk, there are wagons standing ready for departure, the whole of the wagons(inward and outward) must be taken to Thirsk Goods Station and the inward wagons placed at the Standage Point on the return journey.
BR North Eastern Region Sectional Appendix 1960

Above: Looking out from Thirsk Town yard towards the junction on 1st October 1966 with BR 204hp(Class 03) 0-6-0 shunter No. D2077 - of Thornaby - working as Thirsk Yard pilot and trip loco. On this occasion it had brought a brakevan railtour to Thirsk Town for the RCTS to mark the end of this historic terminus - were they the first and only passengers to arrive there since 1855?
Jack Wild/Stephen Chapman archive

Below: A view towards the end of the branch at Thirsk Town in the late 1950s showing the various facilities for handling goods traffic. One of Northallerton's allocation of five BR Standard Class 2 2-6-0s, No. 78010, is doing the honours in the yard.
J.W. Hague/Neville Stead collection

Above: The original terminus of the Leeds & Thirsk Railway at Thirsk Town with the passenger and goods stations as they were on Saturday 1st October 1966. The yard is clear of wagons and the only trains likely to come after this day would be to lift the track and recover the "redundant assets." *Jack Wild/Stephen Chapman archive*

Below: A final view of 78010 shunting at Thirsk Town goods yard in happier times, the late 1950s when the depot was still busy.
J.W. Hague/Neville Stead collection

Above: Back to Melmerby and onto the Masham branch. Sporting Through Freight headlamps, Starbeck-based J39 0-6-0 No. 64861 passes the site of the branch platform at Melmerby station with the pick-up returning from Masham to Ripon in the 1950s. *J.W. Hague/Neville Stead collection*

Below: The outward-bound Masham goods, this time displaying class K headlamp and with a slightly healthier load, pulls away from Melmerby behind Starbeck's NER-vintage Class A6 4-6-2 tank No. 69797 shortly after the formation of British Railways. Another picture of the same train at this spot shows sister loco 9791 in late LNER days carrying Through Freight headlamps as above and with only two wagons plus brake van in tow. *J.W. Hague/Neville Stead collection*

Above: Forget idyllic scenes of Great Western branch lines - the Masham branch encompassed everything about the tranquillity of the English countryside and its branch lines in the late 1950s. J39 0-6-0 No. 64861 is at Nosterfield level crossing, between Tanfield and Melmerby, with the returning Masham goods on the same occasion as the picture opposite. *J.W. Hague/Neville Stead collection*

The 1960 North Eastern Region Sectional Appendix showed the Masham branch to be 7 miles 914 yards long from the junction at Melmerby and worked according to One Engine in Steam regulations. The maximum speed was 25mph with a 10mph restriction over Wath Lane, Nosterfield, Thornborough, Tanfield Gates and Aldborough level crossings at which drivers were instructed to sound their whistle when approaching. All level crossings except Tanfield Gates were operated by train crews.

Right: The scene at Tanfield station on 30th January 1963 where the returning Masham goods has paused to drop off water cans. On this occasion, an extra brake van was attached for a party of RCTS members.
Standing on the platform is driver Harris, the York-based 350hp (Class 08) loco's driver who was due to retire after this day's shift.
Jack Wild/Stephen Chapman archive

Above: Tanfield station looking towards Masham in the 1950s. The signal box stands in the foreground and Tanfield Gates crossing keeper's cabin at the far end of the platform. The iron railings along the back wall of the platform mark the rear of the coal drops. *J.W. Hague/Neville Stead collection*

Tanfield station, which served the village of West Tanfield as well as the surrounding district, was listed in the 1956 Stations Handbook as equipped with a 1.5-ton crane and able to handle parcels(at the passenger station,) general goods, livestock and horse boxes and prize cattle vans. It closed along with the branch line on 11th November 1963.

Below: Masham passenger station and station master's house looking towards the end of the branch in the 1950s. As at Tanfield, Masham remained open for parcels traffic after losing its passenger service in 1931. *J.W. Hague/Neville Stead collection*

SHORT MEMORIES

Easter 1961: Deltic No.D9002 passes Ripon while on a Leeds-Newcastle test run.

Jan. 1962: The value of the railway to Wensleydale is demonstrated when snow blocks local roads. The 7.35am Northallerton-Leyburn parcels with a coach added and extended to Hawes, and back in the afternoon, forms a passenger service so that people can get to market. Between Aysgarth and Redmire it stops alongside farms to pick up milk churns because the usual road collections cannot get through. Ivatt 2-6-0 46475 runs ahead with a snowplough.

10.4.62: A2/3 No.60521 *Watling Street* (52D) works the 11am Liverpool-Newcastle.

Above: By 30th January 1963, the scene at Masham station had become far more depressing, especially when accompanied by the weather of that particular winter. This is the outward view along the station platform towards the signal box with stored wagons by then occupying the road once used by passenger trains. Masham station was on the Ripon-Leyburn road about three quarters of a mile east of the town, on the opposite side of the River Ure.

Below: Sitting in the goods yard on the same day was this elderly 6-wheeled goods van still lettered "N E " on the side. *Both Jack Wild/Stephen Chapman archive*

Above: Masham goods yard, looking west and viewed from the bank leading up to the coal drops, presented a fairly busy scene in the 1950s. The weighbridge house can just be seen between the two lines of vans while the trees beyond mark the site of the works yard for the reservoir construction projects, and the starting point for the narrow gauge line to Colsterdale. *Neville Stead collection*

The 1956 Handbook of Stations listed Masham as equipped with a 1.5-ton crane and able to handle general goods, livestock, horse boxes and prize cattle vans and carriages and motor cars by passenger or parcels train - even though there weren't any passenger or parcels trains by then. In common with most North East branch line termini, Masham also had a small, single-road engine shed leading off a 42ft turntable as well as the pre-fabricated store on the left which was built to supplement the goods shed.
Both pictures J.W. Hague/Neville Stead collection

Below: Looking up to the spot from where the above picture was taken, showing the coal drops, goods shed and station buildings.

Above: It is 30th January 1963, one of the coldest winters in living memory, and staff had to clear the points in Masham yard before the 0-6-0 diesel shunter that has brought the pick-up from Ripon could get to work. The job is now done, the class class K headlamp is in place and the train, complete with extra brake van for an RCTS party, is ready to make its way back to Ripon. Although complete closure is but 10 months away, the yard still looks busy with coal merchants traffic at least. The signal box is on the right, behind the coal bank. *Jack Wild/Stephen Chapman archive*

Below: A heartwarming - and summery - scene for us to remember Masham by - if only we could return just once and see it all again. It was still a busy station in the 1950s when J25 0-6-0 No. 65726 was shunting the pick-up. The loco and its wagons are on the passenger station road and the brake van and its wagons on the coal bank. *J.W. Hague/Neville Stead collection*

Above: Back to Melmerby for the third and final time. This view shows the main, Northallerton line platforms looking south on 20th November 1966. The Thirsk line was over on the left, behind the station buildings, and the Masham branch to the right, behind the platform. Worthy of note is the 55mph permanent speed restriction on the Up line at this spot, showing that this route had quite a high normal line speed. Melmerby closed to passengers on 6th March 1967, being the only other station remaining open north of Harrogate besides Ripon by that time. North of here the line was closed completely but it remained open to a mile south of here to serve the ordnance depot until October 1969. *P.B. Booth/Neville Stead collection.*

Below: Leeds Neville Hill A3 No. 60086 *Gainsborough* has charge of the northbound Queen of Scots as it passes through Melmerby in the 1950s. The Masham branch can be seen on the right. *J.W. Hague/Neville Stead collection*

Above: Just under three miles north of Melmerby station, B16/1 4-6-0 No. 61425 speeds a Down early 1950s express past Sinderby signal box, behind which is the goods yard. By this time, the box was only opened when the pick-up goods required to shunt there. It was completely abolished in September 1955 and replaced by two ground frames, one for the Up sidings and one for the Down sidings.

Below: Photographed from the cattle dock, Neville Hill A3 No. 60081 *Shotover* rolls by with an Up express. Sinderby station served the villages of Kirklington and Ainderby Quernhow besides Sinderby but was at least a mile from each one.
Both J.W. Hague/Neville Stead collection.

The Ripon-Northallerton section of the Leeds Northern was shown in the 1960 BR N. E. Region Sectional Appendix to be signalled by Absolute Block with a maximum line speed of 70mph. Signal boxes(with distance from previous box) were at Littlethorpe(3 miles 133yds from Wormald Green,) Ripon(1 mile 1555yds.,) Melmerby South(1 mile 1560yds.,) Melmerby North(1 mile 53yds.,) Pickhill(4 miles 33 yds.,) Newby Wiske(3 miles 1307yds.,) Cordio Junction(1 mile 1428yds.,) and Boroughbridge Road(1 mile 115yds.)

Additional running lines were an Up Goods Loop at Ripon accommodating 33 wagons, engine and brake van, and a Down Refuge Siding at Melmerby accommodating 15 wagons, engine and brake van. There was also at one time a long siding running south from Cordio Junction for about a mile, loosely following the Up side but deviating slightly away from it in places. It included a run-round loop and siding.

The 1969 Eastern Region(Northern Area) Sectional Appendix showed the remaining 13 miles 297yds-single line from Starbeck North Junction to Melmerby Ground Frame(formerly Melmerby South) to be worked under One Engine in Steam regulations with a maximum speed of 25mph. It was finally closed in late 1969 and deleted from the Sectional Appendix per the 4-weekly notice issued on 14th March 1970.

The Cordio Junction-Boroughbridge Road and Northallerton South(station) sections were still shown in the 1969 Sectional Appendix, two years after complete closure of the Melmerby-Northallerton section, only being deleted per the 4-weekly notice issued on 4th July 1970, the same time as the curve giving direct access from Northallerton station to the Wensleydale line. Unless this was an earlier administrative oversight being corrected, the only obvious purpose for the retention of Cordio Junction and the two lines to it would be so that freight trains coming off the Wensleydale branch could reverse there and go forward to Low Gates and Tees Yard without reversing in Northallerton station and inconveniencing the ECML. Once the Northallerton station-West Junction curve was closed, they propelled from Castle Hills Junction to the station and then went forward via the Northallerton Station-East Junction curve to Tees Yard.

Sinderby was listed in the 1956 Handbook of Stations as equipped to handle general goods, livestock, horse boxes and prize cattle vans, and carriages and motor cars by passenger and parcels train but had no permanent crane. It was downgraded to a public delivery siding when the passenger station closed on 1st January 1962. Also here was a public delivery siding to serve neighbouring Pickhill, known as Pickhill Siding. It was listed as equipped only for coal, mineral and "side to side" traffic in wagon loads.

Despite being closed completely on 11th November 1963 and the track long since removed, the yard only despatched its last train in May 2009 when privately preserved Brush Type 4(Class 47) No. 47540 and a number of coaches which had been stored on the site for six years were moved away to make room for widening of the A1.

Below: Original B16/1 4-6-0 No. 61412 from Neville Hill shed rumbles through Pickhill station, six and three quarter miles south of Northallerton, with an Up heavy Through Freight in the 1950s. At that time, the Leeds Northern south of Northallerton carried a fair amount of freight traffic but most of it was rerouted via York as the final stages of the ECML widening progressed during the 1950s to avoid double heading on the gradients south of Harrogate. Purely a passenger station, Pickhill closed on 14th September 1959. Almost unusually, Pickhill station was close to the village - and only three quarters of a mile from Sinderby. The level crossing here doubtless ensured the retention of its signal box. *J.W. Hague/Neville Stead collection*

SHORT MEMORIES

24.4.62: Royal Scot 4-6-0 No.46161 *King's Own* is noted at Ripon with 3.30pm Manchester Exchange-Newcastle relief. A2/3 No.60513 *Dante*(34E*)* is on the 4.47pm Newcastle-Liverpool.

2.9.63: Sulzer Type 2 No. D5169 paired with a brake tender is on the Hawes pick-up.

31.7.65: A1 Pacifics still well in evidence on the ECML through Northallerton. No. 60134 *Foxhunter* is on an express from London at about 06.15, 60124 *Kenilworth* has taken over a London-bound express at Darlington, and 60118 *Archibald Sturrock* is on a Leeds-Glasgow.

10.65: A1 No. 60151*Midlothian* working regularly through Thirsk during the last week of the month. On 29th it is noted on a 16-coach empty stock train.

Above: Boroughbridge Road Junction in the 1950s. WD 2-8-0 No. 90048 slogs over the level crossing and makes for Longlands Junction and the ECML to York with a Through Freight from Teesside. The engine shed can be seen above the wagons and the main line station is above right. In the foreground is the line to Cordio Junction and Ripon. *Neville Stead collection*

Below: Looking down on Boroughbridge Road level crossing from the main line station on 19th April 1963 with BR/Sulzer Type 2(Class 25) No. D5166 and brake tender en-route with a freight to Teesside. *Rev. David Benson*

Above: With Northallerton engine shed on the left, V2 2-6-2 No. 60932 brings its northbound express over Boroughbridge Road crossing and through the low level platforms. The site of a station used by 19th century local trains from Ripon, the platforms were rebuilt for emergency use in world war two in case the ECML station was blocked by enemy action. Built of earth, old sleepers, corrugated iron and surfaced with ash, they were retained into the 1960s for use by trains diverted due to engineering work. *Neville Stead collection*

Below: The south end of Northallerton shed viewed from the main line station with K1 2-6-0 No. 62048 in residence at 3.20pm on 7th November 1959. *Robert Anderson*

Locomotives allocated to 51J Northallerton, August 1950: D20 4-4-0: 62347/59/88/91; J21 0-6-0: 65030; J25 0-6-0: 65645/93/725; G5 0-4-4T: 67324/44/46; Y3 4wVBT: 68159. Total: 12

Although firmly in Yorkshire, Northallerton shed was coded 51J in BR's Darlington District. Its main purpose was to provide engines for local passenger, goods and pilot workings around the area, but especially on the Wensleydale line. Until 1954, two of its engines were outbased at Leyburn, one for shunting and the other for passenger duty. In common with other small depots in BR's North Eastern Region its allocation of elderly North Eastern locos was replaced by more modern steam types during the early to mid-1950s, notably BR Standard and London Midland & Scottish Railway-design engines. This view by the late Arthur Wilson of the south end shows BR Standard Class 2 2-6-0 No. 78010 at home on 14th October 1956.

One peculiarity of Northallerton depot was that it had no turntable or coaling facilities for its locomotives, being little more than a long two-road straight shed with a couple of standage sidings. The coal stage and turntable were situated up in the high level goods yard at the north end of the main line station which meant engines tripping between the two locations for servicing. The shed staff consisted of only the shedmaster, a fitter and mate, a boiler washer and a labourer.

The shed closed on 4th March 1963 and its remaining seven engines transferred to Darlington though 78010 had a spell in store at York South. The shed was later demolished and a warehouse has long occupied the site.

Below: A full view of Northallerton engine shed, cold and empty, as seen from the main line station in April 1964.
Jack Wild/Stephen Chapman archive

Locomotives allocated to 51J Northallerton, June 1955: D20 4-4-0: 62359; J39 0-6-0: 64978; J25 0-6-0: 65720/26; G5 0-4-4T: 67278/342; BR Standard Class 2 2-6-0: 78010-14. Total: 11

Locomotives allocated to Northallerton, March 1963: K1 2-6-0: 62003/44; BR Standard Class 2 2-6-0: 78010/11/12/14/15. Total: 7

The November 1951 Darlington District working timetable of local engines showed Northallerton shed as having five freight duties. They were: 6am Jervaulx, 8.30am Newport, 10am Hawes, 6.30pm Darlington and 8.40pm Thirsk. The shed provided two pilot engines. The September 1956 Darlington District local freight working book showed No. 1 pilot working 5.20am-6pm daily. "Shunting Northallerton Low and High yards, also passenger station. Transfers or trips as required." No. 2 working 11.30am-6pm(8.10am-2.15pm Sats.) "Shunting at Thirsk Junction and works trips to Thirsk Town as necessary."

Above: WD 2-8-0 No. 90482 takes water at the column just north of the level crossing at Low Gates in spring 1967. *Armstrong Railway Photographic Trust*

LOW GATES SIGNAL BOX. When the locomotive of an Up or Down train requires water during the time the level crossing gates are across the railway, the appropriate subsidiary signal will be lowered when the driver has been brought quite or nearly to a stand at the Home signal, and the driver must stop his locomotive at the water column short of the level crossing gates. The driver must not proceed until he receives a green hand signal from the signalman. *BR Eastern Region Sectional Appendix 1969*

Right: The layout at Northallerton Low as it was in the first half of the 20th century. By the 1970s the six roads south of the goods shed, including the coal drops, had been removed. The passenger station here closed as long ago as 1901 and became the goods station. The 1956 Handbook of Stations listed Low as having a maximum cranage capacity of 5 tons and equipped to handle general goods, livestock, furniture vans, carriages, motor cars, portable engines and machines on wheels. It was reduced to a public delivery siding in 1968. In 2010 just two short sidings remain for engineers and emergency use. There was also a National Cold Sores siding at Northallerton.

The layout at Northallerton demanded a good deal of operational flexibility so that shunting movements could be undertaken efficiently. The 1969 BR Eastern Region Sectional Appendix stated that up to 15 freight wagons may be propelled with or without a brake van in both directions between Boroughbridge Road and Low Gates, though a guard's brake van must be leading in fog or falling snow. Up to six empty coaching stock vehicles or 20 freight wagons could be propelled from Northallerton Station to Low Gates provided the weather was clear, and an undefined number with or without brake van in the opposite direction. Trains could be worked without a brake van in both directions between Low Gates and Boroughbridge Road, and to Low Gates from the station. Should passenger trains booked to call at Northallerton station need to be diverted via Boroughbridge Road and Longlands Junction, they had to be assisted by a pilot locomotive on the rear in both directions between Low Gates and the station. It stated: "The rear locomotive must not assist the train being drawn by pilot locomotive with the train locomotive in rear. The locomotive in rear must be signalled as 'Locomotive assisting in rear of train."

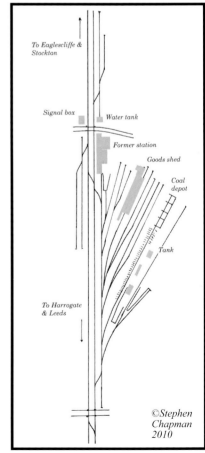

To Eaglescliffe & Stockton

Signal box

Water tank

Former station

Goods shed

Coal depot

Tank

To Harrogate & Leeds

©Stephen Chapman 2010

Above: Low Gates crossing looking towards Stockton on 9th April 1955. The old passenger station, closed in 1901, is on the right and the old signal box on the left with a J25 0-6-0 alongside. *Armstrong Railway Photographic Trust*

Centre: The old Northallerton Low passenger station in February 2010, now a kitchen and bedroom centre. The goods yard was behind the buildings while the two remaining short sidings are out of view on the right. *Stephen Chapman*

Bottom: Having taken water and received the green flag from the signalman leaning out of his window, WD No. 90482 clanks past the new signal box at Low Gates. This one, situated on the opposite side of the line to the old one, between the crossing and the water tank, replaced the old structure in 1956. It remains in use in 2010 but the upper portion has been modernized and since 1997 it has controlled the whole line almost as far north as Eaglescliffe, 14 miles away, where it interfaces with Bowesfield box, Teesside. *Armstrong Railway Photographic Trust*

Above: West Hartlepool J39 0-6-0 No. 64862 looks very smart for the immediate post-war era as it passes an equally well-tended Brompton station with what seems to be the 5.53pm West Hartlepool to Northallerton on 23rd April 1949. This was the engine for the 8.20pm Low Gates-Newport-West Hartlepool goods and was specified a J39 because of the outward passenger working.

Just two and quarter miles north of Northallerton, Brompton was served in summer 1950 by the following weekday trains: 7.25am(7.20 Northallerton-West Hartlepool,) 11.5am(9.17 Leeds-Middlesbrough,) 1.40pm(12.55 Middlesbrough-Northallerton,) 3.45pm(3.40 Northallerton-Stockton/West Hartlepool SO,) 5.16pm (5.11 SX Northallerton-West Hartlepool,) 8.6pm(6.45 West Hartlepool-Northallerton.) There was no Sunday service. By summer 1955 only two trains each way called there and by summer 1960 the only trains calling at Brompton were 7.52am Leeds-Middlesbrough at 9.25 and the 6.12pm Sunderland-York at 7.39, both DMUs. Even so, it hung on until closing to both passengers and goods on 6th October 1965. *Armstrong Railway Photographic Trust*

Brompton goods yard, which was situated south of the station and level crossing, was listed in the 1956 Handbook of Stations as being equipped to handle only general goods and there was no permanent crane. A notable feature here were the linen mills alongside the goods yard though they had no rail connection of their own.

Below: The layout at Welbury as it was in 1963. Not to scale

In summer 1950 Welbury was served by the same passenger trains as Brompton plus the 5.53 West Hartlepool-Northallerton which called there at 6.51. It closed to passengers on 20th September 1954 but stayed open for parcels. Goods facilities were listed in the 1956 Stations Handbook as having a 3-ton crane and able to handle general goods, livestock, horse boxes and prize cattle vans, and carriages and motor cars by passenger or parcels train. There was also a siding two miles further north at West Rounton Gates where the station had closed in 1939. After being reduced to a public delivery siding in June 1961, Welbury closed to goods traffic on 30th September 1963.

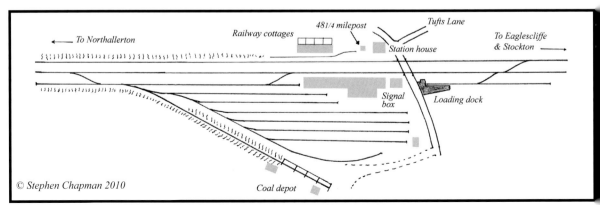

To Northallerton ←
Railway cottages
481/4 milepost
Tufts Lane
To Eaglescliffe & Stockton
Station house
Signal box
Loading dock
Coal depot

© Stephen Chapman 2010

Above: V2 2-6-2 No. 60805 heads a northbound express through Welbury station, 5.5 miles north of Northallerton, in 1949.
Pictures on this page by courtesy of the Armstrong Railway Photographic Trust

Below: Picton station, 10 miles north of Northallerton was where the North Yorkshire & Cleveland line from Whitby via Stokesley and Potto joined the Leeds Northern(see Railway Memories No.18.) Here, A8 4-6-2T No. 69866 of 51D Middlesbrough shed, arrives at the station with a 1950s Stockton to Whitby service. Despite the loss of its Whitby trains in 1954, Picton hung on, being served by Northallerton trains until 4th January 1960 when it closed to passengers. It continued to handle goods traffic until 7th September 1964, being listed in the 1956 Handbook of Stations as equipped to handle all classes of freight but with no permanent crane. The signal box here survived until 1997 when it was abolished under the scheme which brought the line under the control of Low Gates.

Above: Starting out from Northallerton on the afternoon service in the early 1950s, with G5 0-4-4T No. 67312 on the front. *J.W. Hague/Neville Stead collection*

Below: Two and three quarter miles out of Northallerton, we come to Ainderby which served the villages of Ainderby Steeple and Morton-on-Swale and was actually in Morton. Like most Wensleydale stations, it remained open for parcels after the loss of its passenger trains. In 1956 it was also listed as able to handle general goods, livestock and horse boxes and prize cattle vans. Goods facilities were withdrawn on 1st November 1965. This was it, looking west, in the late 1960s, just the single track remaining but with the small timber signal box still a block post. *Neville Stead collection*

Above: A truly evocative branch line scene at Ainderby some time in the early 1950s where the signalman and driver of a G5 0-4-4T on a Northallerton-bound service exchange single line tablets. *J.W. Hague/Neville Stead collection*

Below: Half a mile west of Ainderby station we cross the River Swale by the four-span Morton bridge. D20 4-4-0 No. 62388 completes the scene as it crosses with a Northallerton-bound service. The carriages seem to contain only a few passengers. *J.W. Hague/Neville Stead collection*

Above: Scruton, four and a half miles from Northallerton, in the early 1950s with G5 0-4-4T No. 67345 - known locally as "Old Faithful" - heading a westbound service. Scruton closed to passengers on 26th April 1954 and to goods on 7th May 1956.
J.W. Hague/Neville Stead collection
Below: Scruton on 3rd May 1983 with Brush Type 4 No. 47303 approaching on the limestone train to Redmire. Despite the station's early closure, the level crossing necessitated the retention of staff in the shape of a crossing keeper, seen stood on the former platform. The gate cabin here controlled the signals protecting the crossing but was no longer a block post. *Neville Stead*

Above: Leeming Bar, five and three quarter miles from Northallerton, was one of the more important stations on the line and indeed still is in 2010, being the current headquarters the Wensleydale Railway which has its engine shed and carriage sidings there. It was here that the line changed from single to double track for the mile and three quarters to Bedale and J21 0-6-0 No. 65038 is awaiting the single line to Northallerton. The large building on the left was once the Vale of Mowbray brewery which had its own siding. It later became maltings for brewers Camerons and by the time of this picture was the Vale of Mowbray pork processing factory.
Both pictures J.W. Hague/Neville Stead collection

Below: A fine view of Leeming Bar from the west in the 1950s showing the fair-sized goods shed and, to the right of it, the coal depots. The 1956 Handbook of Stations shows it as equipped to handle parcels and all classes of goods except for carriages and motor cars by passenger or parcels train. It had crane capacity of just 15 hundredweight. Goods facilities were withdrawn on 1st November 1965.

Above: G5 0-4-4T No. 67314 waits at Leeming Bar station with a westbound service, the first three vehicles of which are six-wheeled milk tanks. *J.W. Hague/Neville Stead collection*

Below: At Aiskew level crossing, about half a mile west of Leeming Bar on the double track section to Bedale. K1 2-6-0 No. 62005 crosses the A684 Northallerton-Leyburn road while taking a Stephenson Locomotive Society railtour to Redmire on 20th May 1967. The double track was singled around 1985. *Neville Stead collection*

Above: Bedale goods yard, seen on the left with a Wickham platelayers' trolley present, remained open for almost 30 years after the passenger service had been withdrawn, having been reduced to a public delivery siding in September 1967. Brush Type 4(Class 47) No. 47287 passes the goods shed and pre-fabricated stores as it moves oil tanks through the station while on pick-up duty in April 1977.
Malcolm Roughley/Stephen Chapman archive

Seven and a half miles from Northallerton, Bedale was listed in 1956 as having a one-ton crane and being able to handle parcels and all classes of freight except carriages and motor cars by passenger and parcels train. A private siding served an Esso oil terminal.

Below: Double-heading with a Sulzer Type 2 diesel(Class 25,) K1 No. 62005 returns the 20th May 1967 SLS railtour to Northallerton, passing Bedale signal box and approaching the station as it does. *Neville Stead collection*

Above: Closed to passengers but Bedale is still intact and complete with its platform canopy and horse dock in this 1950s view looking east from the level crossing. *J.W. Hague/Neville Stead collection*

Below: Bedale was the point where the double track from Leeming Bar reverted to single. Here the driver of 47287 collects the tablet from the signalman before proceeding to Leyburn with the pick-up in April 1977. *Malcolm Roughley/Stephen Chapman archive*

SHORT MEMORIES

30.5.67: Jubilee No. 45562 *Alberta* arrives at Ripon with the Royal Train after conveying the Duke of Edinburgh to Nidd Bridge. It runs round and returns to York via Starbeck.

11 & 12.7.67: Withdrawn A4 No. 60019 *Bittern* works York-Newcastle parcels trains through Northallerton.

17.10.70: The 07.17 Newcastle-Norwich consisting of two bogie parcels vans and 8 coaches drawn by Class 40 No. 270 collides at 70mph with a lorry carrying a portable cement mixer across Lowfields Farm occupation crossing, 2.25 miles north of Low Gates. A trackman acting as handsignalman at the crossing is killed and the lorry driver injured.

Above: This was how Bedale station looked when viewed from the signal box on 23rd March 1991. The station buildings and goods shed survive along with the platform and crossing gates but the only track was a single running line. *Stephen Chapman*

Bedale Coal Cell Sidings: Due to the condition of the track, locomotives are prohibited from travelling over the coal cells until further notice. *BR 4-Weekly Notice 7th June 1969.*

Below: Looking west from Bedale station as 47287 shunts oil tanks in the Esso siding while working the pick-up in April 1977. *Malcolm Roughley/Stephen Chapman archive*

Above: After Bedale, we reach Crakehall, nine and three quarter miles from Northallerton and this is how it looked, viewed to the west, when still open for business in the 1950s. There were no goods facilities. *J.W. Hague/Neville Stead collection*

Below: Crakehall looking east on 23rd March 1991. The station building has become a private house and the platform has gone but the canopy survives while the level crossing gates have been replaced by train crew-operated booms. *Stephen Chapman*

Above: Having passed Jervaulx, a mile and three quarters from Crakehall, we are now at Finghall Lane, thirteen and a quarter miles from Northallerton. This view shows the station looking east in the early 1950s. This station closed to goods as well as passengers on 26th April 1954. *Both pictures J.W. Hague/Neville Stead collection*

Below: This wonderfully rustic and utterly charming scene shows J21 0-6-0 No. 65038 departing Finghall Lane with what looks like the Sunday afternoon train to Leyburn, complete with milk tank and one passenger coach but not stopping for goat's milk.

Above: Now fourteen and a quarter miles from Northallerton we move deeper into the Wensleydale heartland and arrive at Constable Burton. This is how it looked in the early 1950s with G5 No. 67314 arriving on a westbound service.

Below: Nothing may remain in 2010 of Constable Burton station, about half a mile south of the village and Burton Hall estate, but it was once an important passing place. In this early 1950s scene, J21 No. 65038 waits patiently as G5 No. 67345 prepares to leave. The time could be either 8am or, more likely, 4.49pm, for those were the times when two passenger trains were booked to pass here - assuming both these are passenger trains. This station was listed in 1956 as equipped to handle parcels, general goods, livestock and horse boxes and prize cattle vans but despite boasting a 10-ton crane, it closed to goods traffic in October 1957. *Both J.W. Hague/Neville Stead colln.*

Above: Just east of Leyburn was Harmby Quarry, at one time one of the line's biggest sources of mineral traffic. This is Harmby East, the east-facing connection to the quarry sidings. The quarry is now a caravan and camp site. *J.W. Hague/Neville Stead collection*

Below: Brush Type 4 No. 47287 runs into Leyburn station with the pick-up to Redmire, now formed entirely of mineral wagons, in April 1977. On the left is the site of the engine shed and on the right the lines into the then, still active goods yard.
Malcolm Roughley/Stephen Chapman archive

Above: The market town of Leyburn, 17.5 miles from Northallerton, is the main centre of Wensleydale and its small station presents a big station atmosphere on 27th March 1954 as G5 No. 67314 takes water at the westbound platform. *Neville Stead collection*

Below: Wensleydale passenger trains were mainly worked by Northallerton-based G5 0-4-4 tanks, D20 4-4-0s and J21 0-6-0s. One of the latter, No. 65038 simmers in the station with the 3pm to Hawes. Behind it is the engine shed. It has long since gone but the enginemen's houses on the left of the above picture still stand along with the station which, with Leeming Bar, Bedale, Finghall and Redmire, again sees passenger trains thanks to the Wensleydale Railway. *J.W. Hague/Neville Stead collection*

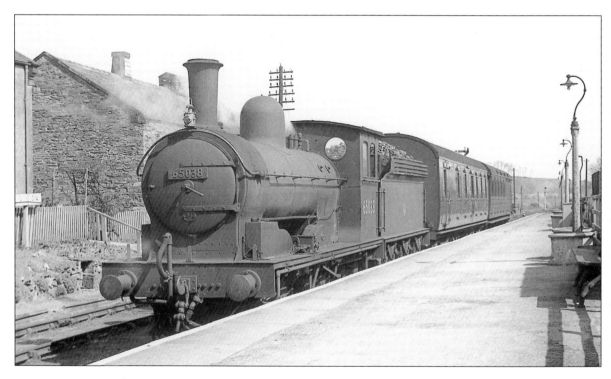

Above: The branch terminus from 1855 to 1873, Leyburn was blessed with a single road engine shed which closed in 1915 but reopened in 1939. Facilities included a 42ft 4 inch turntable but coaling had to be performed by a man shovelling coal from a wagon brought up alongside the locomotive. A sub-shed of Northallerton, it was normally home to two 51J engines outbased there. One was a Class Y3 Sentinel vertical-boilered loco used for local shunting and attaching milk tanks to passenger trains, such as No. 68182 seen here simmering outside the shed on 19th April 1954. The other was a passenger engine whose duties included the first train up to Northallerton in a morning(at 7.52 in 1950,) and the last train back in the evening(due in Leyburn at 10.5pm.)

In the early 1950s G5 0-4-4T No. 67345 was the Leyburn passenger engine(though 67346 was allocated there in August 1950) and Y3 No. 68159 the shunting engine. The end of passenger services in April 1954 rendered the shed redundant and it was demolished in the 1960s. *Neville Stead collection*

Below: The layout at Leyburn as it was in 1913. *Not to scale*

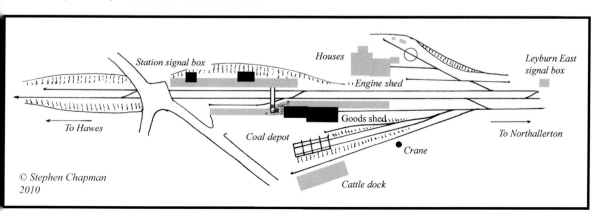

Leyburn's regular shunting loco, Y3 No. 68159 in the station platform on 23rd May 1950. It is displaying station pilot headlamps - not express passenger!
L.A. Strudwick

The Wensleydale line was single track throughout except for a short double track section between Leeming Bar and Bedale.

The BR Eastern Region 1969 Sectional Appendix showed the Wensleydale line, which since 1964 had extended only from Northallerton to Redmire, to be worked by Absolute Block between Leeming Bar and Bedale, as Single line with No Token between Northallerton and Ainderby, by Electric Token between Bedale and Wensley, and One Engine in Steam between Wensley and Redmire.

There were still signal boxes that were block posts at(with distances from previous box) Ainderby(2 miles 1352yds from Northallerton,) Leeming Bar(2 miles 1631yds,) Bedale(1 mile 1329yds,) Leyburn(9 miles 1436yds,) and Wensley(2 miles 1633yds.) Redmire was 2 miles 132yds from Wensley.

The maximum line speed between Northallerton and Wensley was 45mph and 25mph between Wensley and Redmire.

The Leeming Bar-Bedale double track section was listed in "Table K2" as being a line equipped for passenger train working even though there was no booked service.

Additional running lines were at Bedale(Up Refuge Siding able to hold 40 wagons, engine and brake van and Up Goods Loop able to hold 8 wagons, engine and brake van,) Leyburn(Crossing Loop able to hold 57 wagons, engine & van, Up Refuge Siding able to hold 53 wagons, engine and van, and Down Refuge Siding able to hold 34 wagons, engine and van,) and at Wensley(Crossing Loop able to hold 31 wagons, engine and van and Up Refuge Siding able to hold 28 wagons, engine and van.)

The Castle Hills Curve from Northallerton Station to West Junction(formerly Castle Hills Inner Jn.) was worked as a "Single Line with no Token" with West Junction controlled by Northallerton power box. It was 565yds in length and had a maximum line speed of 15mph.

Within 18 months, some rationalisation had taken place which altered the way the line was worked. The Up Refuge Siding at Leyburn was taken out of use per the 4-weekly notice dated 7th June 1969. The 4-weekly notice issued on 14th March 1970 stated the line had been reduced to One Train Working - the new term for One Engine in Steam since the end of steam - between Leyburn and Redmire with the abolition of Wensley signal box and a reduction in line speed to 25mph. The line speed between Northallerton and Leyburn remained at 45mph.

The 4-weekly notice dated 31st July 1970 showed the Castle Hills Curve as taken out of use meaning that trains would in future have to reverse at Castle Hills Junction when entering or leaving the branch. Subsequent reductions took place during the 1980s and 1990s until the remaining signal boxes were abolished, additional running lines removed and the whole 22 miles operated by One Train Working.

The summer 1950 timetable advertised a Monthly Return ticket from Leyburn to King's Cross as costing £3 4s 4d third class and £4 16s 6d first class. From Aysgarth it was £3 6s 3d third class and £4 19s 5d first class. London fares were not advertised in the timetable from any other Wensleydale stations.

Above: Leyburn, still pretty much intact and fully signalled on 16th September 1978 when visited by a York-Redmire DMU excursion operated by BR and the Yorkshire Dales National Park Committee. The Up Crossing Loop is on the right and the goods shed and goods yard, still very much alive years after most others at such small stations across the country had closed, are on the left. Leyburn was listed in 1956 as having a 5-ton crane and able to handle parcels and all classes of freight except carriages and motor cars by passenger or parcels train. Private sidings served the Express Dairy and Ord &Madison's quarry between Leyburn and Wensley. The goods yard was downgraded to a public delivery siding in 1969. *Stephen Chapman*

Below: As with other country goods yards surviving beyond the 1960s it was deliveries to coal merchants which kept Leyburn going. Brush Type 4 No. 47287 pushes a loaded wagon up onto the coal drops while on the pick-up working in April 1977. The coal traffic ended and the goods yard closed in 1982 when BR sought to end the use of loose-coupled, unfitted wagons and began withdrawing the mineral wagons which carried the coal to merchants' depots like this. *Malcolm Roughley/Stephen Chapman archive*

What a difference 13 years makes. This was Leyburn looking east on 23rd March 1991. By this time the only regular traffic was the one limestone train a day from Redmire and consequently the whole place had been stripped to just a single running line. The signal box(originally Leyburn East) which stood at the far end of the station area has gone along with all the sidings, points and signals. Standing defiant amid the desolation are the goods shed and station buildings which were once the headquarters of the Bedale & Leyburn Railway Company which built them and had its boardroom on the first floor. The Down passenger platform was at the far end of the station while the inset on the right, nearest the camera, was the Express Dairy loading dock. The remains of the Up platform are just visible through the trees in the left foreground. *Stephen Chapman*

LEYBURN STATION. The section between Leyburn and Wensley is worked in accordance with the Regulations for Train Signalling on Single Lines by the Electric Token Block System.

An auxiliary Key Token instrument is installed at Leyburn Down Starting signal to enable drivers to obtain a token for the section.

When it is necessary for a driver to receive a token from the Auxiliary instrument the signalman must, after obtaining permission from the signalman at Wensley in the usual way, withdraw the special key from the instrument in the signal box, place it in the slot at the side of the token instrument, give it one half turn to the right, and press the plunger which will cause the indicator on the Auxiliary instrument at the signal to show FREE.

When a train is about to depart the driver must, if not in possession of a token, proceed to the Auxiliary Token instrument referred to, and unless the indicator on the instrument shows FREE he must communicate with the signalman by means of the telephone. When the indicator on the instrument shows FREE a token must be extracted from the instrument in accordance with the instructions shown on the brass plate fixed to the instrument.

After the token has been obtained from the instrument the driver must advise the signalman accordingly on the telephone and place the token in the usual leather pouch, and the signalman must pass the special key by way of the slot into the token instrument. Tokens cannot be replaced in the Auxiliary Instrument. Should it be necessary to cancel a token which has been withdrawn from the Auxiliary instrument, this should be done by returning the token to the signalman at Leyburn.

BR Eastern Region Sectional Appendix 1969

SHORT MEMORIES

17.9.77: The Yorkshire Dales National Park Committee runs two return "Dalesrail" trains between Newcastle and Redmire calling at Bedale and Leyburn. More specials are run over the next 4 years.

2.1.93: A 13-coach railtour from London expected to be the last train on the Wensleydale line is worked to Redmire by English Electric Type 3s 37714 and 37885.

6.9.94: A DMU is deliberately crashed into a car on Yafforth crossing near Ainderby to demonstrate the danger of motorists flouting safety rules.

WORKING OF WENSLEY QUARRY. When empty wagons are being placed in the South Durham Steel & Iron Co. Ltd.'s siding the train must be divided on the main line and the wagons placed in the appropriate sidings in accordance with the accommodation available. *BR Eastern Region Sectional Appendix 1969*

Above: On to Wensley, two and a half miles and six minutes from Leyburn, 20 miles from Northallerton and serving the village which gives its name to the whole dale. A few hundred yards before the station were the connections to Wensley Quarry, once the line's biggest source of limestone traffic and as can be seen, there are a good few large hopper wagons in the siding on the right. There is still a big quarry between Wensley and Leyburn in 2010 but not generating rail traffic. Wensley station is just visible in the distance.
Both pictures J.W. Hague/Neville Stead collection

Below: Both Wensley and Redmire quarry sidings were once connected to their quarries by aerial ropeways. This is the loading chute and ropeway mechanism at Wensley, clearly disused by the time of this picture. The buckets and horizontal winding wheel are clearly visible - another treasure of the industrial age lost to our sanitized hi-tec, road-obsessed and uninspiring times.

Above: G5 No. 67312 rolls past the squat Wensley signal box and into the station with a train for Hawes. The platforms here were staggered and the Up platform can be seen beyond the level crossing. In the foreground are the connections to the small goods yard which in 1956 was listed as being able to handle general goods only while the station still handled parcels. Wensley's goods yard survived as a public delivery siding until complete closure in July 1967. *J.W. Hague/Neville Stead collection*

Below: Wensley in April 1977 when viewed from the cab of 47287 waiting to proceed to Redmire. Although the signal box still standing on the left closed in 1970, the crossing loop is still there which is intruiging on a line worked to One Train Only regulations. A member of the train crew now has to manually operate the crossing which at some time since the picture above has been converted from gates to the booms so often favoured in the North East. The station platform and buildings remain intact but on the right, beyond the crossing, the connections into Wensley goods yard had gone some time before. *Malcom Roughley/Stephen Chapman archive*

Above: It is 23rd March 1991 and the robust yet attractive exterior of Wensley station has barely changed except that the platform line has been lifted, a loop no longer required. *Stephen Chapman*

Below: With Castle Bolton just visible through the haze in the distance, Brush Type 5 No. 60038 *Bidean Nam Bian* - then almost brand new - passes Preston-under-Scar with the Redmire-Tees limestone train on 26th April 1991. Such main line freight can still be seen on the Wensleydale Railway to Redmire in the shape of the occasional train carrying army vehicles. *Stephen Chapman*

Above: We have now travelled 22 miles from Northallerton, it's taken 72 minutes and we are at Redmire, the line's terminus since 1964. G5 No. 67345 passes an array of North Eastern slotted signals as it heaves a van and two wooden-bodied coaches past the signal box and on their way back to Northallerton. Beyond the station are the quarry sidings and loading hopper. *Both J.W. Hague/N.Stead colln.*

Below: Redmire station looking east. The wagons up on the coal drops beyond the station buildings indicate the position of the general goods yard while a poster on the station shows a Britannia Pacific in full flight. Another 1950s icon is the classic BBC TV aerial.

Above: Redmire station probably never saw as many passengers as when BR ran its excursions in the late 1970s. The crowded platform is seen here following the arrival of the refurbished "white & bright" DMU from York on 16th September 1978. *Stephen Chapman*

Below: A picture which captures fully the operation of the modernized loading hopper at Redmire . No aerial ropeway but a tipper lorry backing onto a gantry - fascinating in its own way. English Electric Type 1s(Class 20s) Nos. 20173 and 20172 turned out by Thornaby depot in spotless BR blue livery with red solebars and Kingfisher emblems, have charge of the fulls to Tees Yard on 19th November 1986. *Neville Stead*

Above: The stone sidings at Redmire date from 1920 when they were established for the Redmire Limestone Company's quarry and this how they were, looking west, in the 1950s by which time the quarry belonged to steel giant Dorman Long. The loading hopper with its horizontal winding wheel for the aerial ropeway on the top dominates the scene while an ex-North Eastern Railway high capacity hopper wagon stands in the right foreground. In those days there were also connections at the west end which were later removed.

Below: In full flight, the aerial ropeway which brought stone from Redmire quarry to the loading hopper.
Both J.W. Hague/Neville Stead collection

LEYBURN TO REDMIRE. The line between Leyburn and Redmire is worked in accordance with One Train Only regulations. The two Ground Frames at Wensley Lime Company Sidings and the one at Redmire are released by an Annetts key which is fitted to the train Staff provided. A Railman will accompany each train between Leyburn and Wensley in each direction and will be responsible for operating the level crossing gates at Wensley. The Staff is kept at Leyburn Station signal box when not in use. This was an amendment to the 1969 BR Eastern Region Sectional Appendix given in the 4-weekly notice issued on 14th March 1970 upon the reduction of the Leyburn-Wensley section to One Train Working. The Appendix had stated that the line between Wensley and Redmire was worked according to One Engine in Steam regulations, referred to only the one ground frame at Redmire and that the Staff was kept in Wensley signal box.

Redmire was listed in the 1956 Handbook of Stations as having a one-ton crane and equipped to handle parcels and all classes of freight except carriages and motor cars by passenger or parcels train. After being reduced to a public delivery siding in 1959, the goods yard managed to stay in business until 3rd August 1970 when the station closed completely.

Above: The end of the line - beyond here there has been no railway since 1964. Brush Type 4 No. 47287 waits by the loading hopper to pick up loaded wagons in April 1977. This was before the operation had been modernized with the new hopper wagons seen on pages 103 and 105. The brake van was used to the end of this traffic due to the propelling movement at Northallerton.
Malcolm Roughley/Stephen Chapman archive

Below: Moving on three more miles we come to Aysgarth, famous for its cataracts on the River Ure. Here, D20 No. 62372 arrives with the afternoon Hawes to Northallerton service in the early 1950s. The 1956 Stations Handbook listed Aysgarth as having a two-ton crane and able to handle parcels and all classes of freight except carriages and motor cars by passenger or parcels train. It closed along with Askrigg and Hawes when the line shut completely on 27th April 1964, the goods yard a public delivery siding since 1959. *N. Stead colln.*

Above: Askrigg looking north on 9th March 1959 with K1 2-6-0 No. 62005 shunting the Hawes-bound pickup. The 1956 Handbook of Stations listed Askrigg as having a two-ton crane and the ability to handle parcels, general goods, livestock and horse boxes and prize cattle vans. Along with Leyburn, Aysgarth and Hawes, it was one of just four stations on the line with a goods shed. Askrigg primary school stands large in the background with the village beyond. *Chris Gammell/Photos from the Fifties*

Below: The old nameboard on the station's only platform displays the full name of Askrigg for Bainbridge(Bainbridge is about two miles behind the photographer across the fields and the River Ure) as a solitary passenger prepares to board the Northallerton train being brought in by 67345. *J.W. Hague/Neville Stead collection*

Above: Hawes, 34 miles and around an hour and a half from Northallerton, was one of the most important stations on the line serving as it did the centre of the Dales. A train displaying class A headlamps was indeed a rarity and with two roads through the platforms(one a crossing loop) Hawes looks to have ideas above its station as K1 2-6-0 No. 62063 thunders an eastbound special through the Midland/NER joint station. *Neville Stead collection*

Below: D20 4-4-0 No. 62347 stands in Hawes station on 24th April 1954, the last day of services from Northallerton.
Fifty five years later, a Robert Stephenson & Hawthorns industrial 0-6-0 tank, built in 1955(works No. 7845) can be found in Hawes station masquerading as G5 No. 67345 with three coaches, both lines having been reinstated through the platforms, the station now being part of the Dales Countryside Museum. *J.W. Hague/Neville Stead collection*

Left: At Hawes, the line became more London Midland in character, especially after the passenger trains from Northallerton had been withdrawn. Not only that but he LM Region service of just one return train a day from Garsdale kept Hawes station open for five more years.

Known locally as "Bonnyface," the Garsdale train stands in Hawes station with Fairburn 2--6-4T No. 42132 raring to go.

The station buildings are pure Midland Railway, as is the signal box in the distance. A milepost at the far end of the platform declared 262 and three quarter miles from St. Pancras.

Neville Stead collection

Below: Rebuilt B16 4-6-0 No. 61435, destined to be the last B16 of all - and how lamentable that she then went for scrap - runs round her RCTS railtour from Leeds at the east end of Hawes station on 25th April 1964 where her passengers have taken over the cattle dock, not to mention the track. *Jack Wild/Stephen Chapman archive*

Hawes was listed in the 1956 Stations Handbook as having a maximum crane capacity of one and a half tons and the ability to handle all classes of freight. It closed to passengers on 16th March 1959 when the Garsdale section closed completely, and to goods on 27th April 1964 when the section from Redmire closed completely.

Above: The further west we go on the Wensleydale line the more rugged the landscape becomes. Ex-Midland Railway 4F 0-6-0 No. 43893 storms out of Mossdale Head Tunnel with the returning Garsdale-Hawes pick-up. The LMS 1937 Midland Division Sectional Appendix stated that the Hawes branch was six miles 132yds long and worked by Staff and Ticket. *J.W. Hague/Neville Stead collection*

Below: Some of us on today's Settle & Carlisle trains may gaze wistfully out of the window and across to the trackless embankment curving away to the east as we leave Garsdale, trying to imagine it all those years ago with a train on it. And this is the vision we hope to conjure up - D20 No. 62373 approaching journey's end at Garsdale in the early 1950s. *E.E. Smith/Neville Stead collection*

Left: Garsdale was famous for the stockade surrounding its turntable, built to prevent high winds from blowing the engine round and round - as had been known to happen. The loco being turned on this occasion was Ivatt Class 2 2-6-2T No. 41206 which was on Hawes branch duty. The turntable pit can still just be made out on the Down side of the Settle & Carlisle line north of the station but the stockade is long gone. *J.W. Hague/Neville Stead collection*

Below: Journey's end and just under 40 miles from Northallerton, G5 No. 67314, rests at the Hawes face of the island platform on the Up side at Garsdale on 27th March 1954. Originally named Hawes Junction, then Hawes Junction & Garsdale until 1933, Garsdale was, like Pilmoor, a station whose purpose was purely for interchange between branch line and main line. The small community it did serve consisted mainly of railway staff and isolated farms and homesteads. It was at one time the focal point of social life with a small library of around 200 books donated by two sisters in the main waiting room and a meeting room for local functions under the water tank. There was an engine shed here for locomotives working the Northallerton service but it was closed in 1939 when Leyburn reopened.
Garsdale station is still open to passengers in 2010, having survived the 1980s closure threat to the whole Settle & Carlisle line and trains still use the two main line platforms to the left. But the island platform canopy shown here was removed in 1957 and it has also been stripped of most of its buildings and all track on the Hawes side. Some sidings at the far north end remain but see little use.
Neville Stead collection